Policeman'

Harry Cole was born and brought up in Bermondsey, south London. He left school when he was fourteen, during the war, and became a cricket-bat maker, soldier, stonemason and, in 1952, a policeman. For thirty years, until his retirement in 1983, he served at the same police station in London.

He is a qualified FA coach (he has run numerous junior football teams), a referee and a keen cricketer. For many years he had a regular column in the *Warren*, the police magazine. His other books are *Policeman's Progress*, *Policeman's Patch*, *Policeman's Patrol*, *Policeman's Prelude* and *Policeman's Story*, his two-volume autobiography, *Policeman's Gazette* and *The Blue Apprentices*, a novel.

In 1978 Harry Cole was awarded the British Empire Medal for voluntary work. Since leaving the force, in addition to writing he has taken up after-dinner speaking.

Harry Cole

Policeman's Lot

FONTANA/Collins

First published in Great Britain
in 1981 by Fontana Paperbacks,
8 Grafton Street, London W1X 3LA
Eighth impression October 1989

Printed and bound in Great Britain by
William Collins Sons & Co. Ltd, Glasgow

The views expressed in this book are the author's own
and do not necessarily reflect the official views of
the Metropolitan Police

To the men and women of
the Metropolitan Police

Contents

The Block

The early turn parade is never a very lively affair. 5.45 a.m. is not a time to be jolly, and usually the beat postings, traffic points and local informations are only acknowledged with a reluctant grunt. That cold, foggy January morning was no exception. There was a brand-new recruit on parade and he had been placed under my care for the day. I was still green enough to be quite pleased about this. Recruits are always sent out with an older PC for about a month, and usually no one wants them. Older coppers come up with all sorts of excuses, but men younger in service are inclined to accept them in a quietly pleased fashion. In a way it is a sign that you have arrived. For the first time since you have been in the force, there is going to be someone who thinks you are an 'old sweat'. Today it was my turn to teach a recruit the manor. I was quite looking forward to it. With any luck I'd bore the pants off him.

'604!'

'Sergeant!' I replied.

'Besides the recruit, there's a bail message for you to deal with.' He glanced down at the note in his hand. 'Twenty-one Bridewell Dwellings, O'Shaughnessy again. He's been nicked at Bow Street for drunk and indecent and they require a surety. See if his wife'll stand bail.'

'Sergeant,' I answered.

All in all, the morning was not starting too badly. I not only had a recruit to preach to, but I had the O'Shaughnessys and 'the Block' to describe to him. I felt comfortably smug.

Patrick O'Shaughnessy was easy to explain. He was a first-class, incorrigible drunk. If he'd been around the United States during prohibition he would have become the greatest booze smuggler of all time. All that he need have done was to smuggle himself over each state border and wring himself out on arrival. He could have filled the Chicago Lakes on his own.

Bridewell Dwellings, on the other hand, would take a whole day to summarize. They were virtually indescribable. A four-storey Victorian slum that reeked of decay and despair. London was still in the grip of an appalling housing shortage and Bridewell Dwellings marginally had the edge on a park bench. There was one toilet between two families, the roofs leaked, the stone staircases were death-traps, and cats and rats abounded. They were damp, they were insanitary and they were evil. No human being should ever have had to live in them. But people did – and it took its toll. The Block was a boiling-pot of discontent. This discontent manifested itself in an almost universal anti-police feeling. The police weren't like the council, you didn't need an appointment, they were the establishment. You called them and they came. Your immediate emotions could be vented on them. There were occasions when I entered Bridewell Dwellings feeling like a member of an army of occupation.

Yet there were marvellous people in the Block. The fact that they lived there, slept there, loved there, raised kids there and never actually went mad there spoke volumes for their character, dignity and pride. Many, of course, did go under, some mentally, some physically. Some became vicious criminals, others became O'Shaughnessys. One thing was for sure, a call to Bridewell Dwellings was always an adventure and never, never dull.

I explained this to my protégé – David Robins – as we threaded our way through the narrow Walworth streets. Mrs O'Shaughnessy would say her usual 'I don't want the drunken bastard back here!' but some time during the morning she would undergo her customary change of mind. Patrick would incur his usual 'one day or ten shillings' penalty for urinating in the streets, and by midday he would be home. Lunchtime would see the whole ridiculous circus begin again.

We turned into Bridewell Row where the grey, forbidding block dominated one whole side of the street. Opposite the dwellings was a small playpark. Its swings, slides and roundabouts always looked particularly sad on foggy, dark mornings. As I glanced across the park, it seemed the fog was thicker here than in any other street we had passed. Looking skywards, I realized why: someone in the Block had a chimney fire. These fires were fairly common and not at all popular. Apart from the obvious noise and upheaval of the brigade arriving, there was the additional problem of water – and Bridewell Dwellings were considered damp enough. Any water used to douse the fire would usually permeate its way at least two floors below. If you wished to become extremely unpopular you couldn't do better than live near the top of Bridewell Dwellings and sustain a chimney fire.

'We'll have a look at that before we do this message,' I informed young Robins.

The smoke appeared to be coming from one of the chimneys at the end of the street. It was in this section that the O'Shaughnessys lived. We climbed the steep stairs and on the second floor the smell of smoke was noticeably stronger. I crouched at the letter boxes of each of the four doors, sniffing like a bloodhound. It required no great nose to realize that number 12 was definitely sooty. I knocked loudly and, I suppose, rather officiously. After a short delay, I heard a timid female voice.

'Who is it?'

'Police.'

Another delay, then a bolt was slid, a key was turned

and the door partially opened. A tousled blonde head, with yesterday's make-up, peeped around the door. This front door led immediately into the living room. Beyond the living room was the bedroom; just disappearing into it was a bare male bum.

'Yes?' said the tousled head.

'You've got a chimney fire, luv.'

'Oh! Have I?'

She turned and faced back into the room, opening the door wider as she did so.

The first thing I noticed was her attire. Apart from goose pimples, she wore nothing but a short, black, transparent, baby-doll nightie. The second most obvious fact was the fireplace. On the floor immediately in front of the fire was a mattress. The fire itself was encased into its basket by a tightly fitting piece of smouldering hardboard.

I ran quickly across the room and pulled the board away. Immediately there was a blow-back of sparks and smoke.

'Quick! Give me some water!' I ordered as I bent forward to look up the chimney.

After the initial surge, it appeared that the fire was confined solely to the soot at the rear of the grate. Provided we could extinguish that, it should not be too troublesome.

'Here y'are!'

I turned from the fireplace to see the woman was holding a *cup* of water. I had no desire to be offensive but she somehow looked utterly ridiculous, standing there in her sexy nightie, offering a small cup of water to an irate copper who was trying to put out a fire!

'That's no bloody good! Haven't you got a bucket?'

Dave Robins, finally taking his eyes from her breasts, quickly tipped out some crockery from a white-enamelled bowl. The pieces clattered into the sink. He filled the bowl to its brim and carried it across the bare linoed floor.

Experience had taught me that one puts out these sorts of fires a little bit at a time. Dave had no such experience. Before I could stop him he'd hurled the entire contents of the bowl on to the fire. There was the hiss of a thousand angry snakes and we were both immediately covered by a soggy white ash. Steam billowed into the room and up the chimney. The fire certainly appeared out but we were in a dreadful mess.

The blonde almost hurled herself upon me, brushing me down frantically with her hands.

'I'm sorry! I'm sorry!' she kept repeating. 'Just look at your uniforms.'

In different circumstances, I might possibly have enjoyed it, but with each 'brush' she smeared the grey, wet smuts into an all-over paste. I leapt back yelling:

'You silly cow!'

'I'm sorry! I'm sorry!' was all she could say.

She turned to Dave, who was still looking down at his brand-new uniform in sheer disbelief. In a flash she was on to him. Another quick rub down, another clayman.

I undid my tunic pocket and pulled out my notebook and pen.

'What's your name, luv?' I asked.

'Why? You're not nicking me, are you?'

'Even though you deserve it, no. But I do have to make out a fire report. Now, what's your name?' I repeated.

'Do you have to?' she pleaded.

I was beginning to waver; naked blondes in short see-through nighties tend to make me indecisive.

'Well, it's not going to cost you anything, if that's what you're worried about.'

'It's not that. It's well – well, it's 'im,' she said, jerking her thumb in the direction of the bedroom.

Of course! The bum! I'd completely forgotten about him.

'Well, what's the matter with him, don't he like fires?'

'He lives downstairs, that's what,' she answered.

'Oh! I see,' I said, the penny finally dropping.

'Well, I don't!' interrupted David Robins.

A quick explanation followed: every weekday morning, the husband of the blonde left for work punctually at six o'clock. As he went down the staircase, the bloke in the flat below, equally punctually, came up. It was very cold that day, but the lovers had an aversion to performing in the bedroom. She said it made her feel guilty. Therefore all the action took place on the floor in front of the dying embers of the previous night's fire. They were in the habit of fixing the hardboard to the fireplace to liven up the fading coals. Unfortunately, the chimney had ignited before the fire did. I looked at the charred hardboard and wondered how they could have failed to see it, or smell it.

I took the gent's clothing that had been put in a pile beside the mattress, into the bedroom. I dumped it on to the lap of a forlorn, blanket-clad figure sitting in a chair.

'There y'are, mate. I suggest you get dressed and leg it.'

He nodded.

'If they'd been at it for a few more minutes,' said Dave, 'they'd have burst into flames themselves.'

I resisted saying, 'hot stuff, eh', thinking it would not be in keeping with my new image as a mature, experienced policeman, and climbed the next two flights to number 21. I rat-tat-tatted the door knocker and it opened surprisingly quickly. A gaunt, haggard creature with hardly a remnant of the beauty in the twenty-year-old photograph behind her, stood before us. She wore a faded blue pinafore dress held together by three safety pins. I did not need to say a word.

'Where is it this time?' she said wearily.

'Bow Street, luv.'

'What is it?'

'Drunk and indecent. Not serious, just urinating in the streets.'

'Well, he can rot there.' Her voice rose with each syllable. 'I'm not having that drunken bastard back home here again!'

'Okay, luv, I'll tell 'em.'

She crashed the door shut as we picked our way down the staircase in silence. As we entered the comparative sweetness of a foggy, soot-laden Walworth Street, Dave looked thoughtfully at me and murmured:

'They didn't say anything about this at training school.'

'They never do,' I replied. 'You see, there's only one Bridewell Dwellings and if you're at this nick for any length of time, it'll bloody well haunt you.'

'Thanks,' he muttered.

Bridewell Dwellings really did haunt me for all of my service, and in a most peculiar manner. Every time I embarked on a new undertaking, or used some new equipment, so fate always directed me back to the Block. Take, for instance, the day I finally returned from numerous police driving courses at Hendon, passed out as an area car driver. I badly needed my first bandit chase. In spite of all the practices at Hendon, it is the true-life chase that really counts. In and out of the morass of London's traffic: twisting; turning; accelerating; braking; always in command of the car. At least, that is the theory the student is taught at the school; but no matter how expertly one may perform on the skid pan, what will happen the first time I race down the wet Walworth Road? I was into my fourth month of driving the area car when it finally happened.

Travelling towards me in a black Ford saloon were two young men aged about twenty. As they were about to pass, we gave them just a cursory glance, but then the driver rubbed his face! Now if someone is going to glimpse your face for just a fleeting second and you don't wish him to – you always rub your face. You really have no choice. An innocent enough move, but what a betrayal! I swung the car into a swift 'U' turn and almost immediately the lights of the Ford were extinguished. We were off!

Within a couple of minutes, I had secured a position about thirty yards behind the bandit car. I knew he couldn't shake me off and, after several attempts, so did he. All I had to do was remain in that position: time was on my side, soon he would make a mistake. He drove finally into a cul-de-sac. This was no accident, he obviously knew the area very well. It was fairly obvious that the occupants intended to run for it, via the alley at the end of the street.

The Ford slowed dramatically and before the car came to a halt both occupants had jumped. The passenger immediately slipped and was easily caught by my radio operator. The driver, however, was away like a long dog. I was currently playing three games of football a week and I did not anticipate too much of a problem. On the other hand, he did have some forty yards' start and, with the certainty of being nicked if he faltered, his incentive was infinitely greater than mine.

We ran through numerous streets and flats and, in addition, we climbed two fences. I was nearing exhaustion. The only thing that kept me going was that the distance between us had halved. He at least had to be as tired as I was. Finally, at little more than walking pace, he turned into Bridewell Row. 'Where else?' I thought. Slowly jogging into the first block's entrance, he was immediately out of sight. Just as I entered the building I was almost knocked down by a man leaving; he was pushing a large pram and acknowledged me with an unusually friendly nod. All the stair flights in Bridewell contained seven steps, except the first staircase which contained fourteen. As I had negotiated the man with the pram I'd thought I heard a door slam somewhere above me. I put on a new spurt and raced up the first few steps. My knees suddenly began to quiver and almost involuntarily I stopped dead. He just couldn't have made it up that staircase. There just wasn't sufficient time. But where had he gone?

The pram! Of course! But where had he taken it from? I had never at any time seen his face; in fact, all he had ever been to me was a shadowy figure running in the dark. I jumped down the few remaining stairs and reached the pavement. I called to the pram-pusher who was now casually sauntering some forty yards away.

'Oy, mate! You with the pram! Just a minute!'

I did not accomplish this easily. It was interspersed with pants, coughs and numerous deep breaths.

'Yerse,' came back a high falsetto voice.

When I reached him, I could barely breathe at all. He, on the other hand, appeared totally relaxed. In fact he was breathing so slightly I could scarcely hear it.

'What do you want?' he asked.

Before I could say another word, he exploded in a fit of terrifying coughing. He fell backwards and sat on the kerbside. He was gasping for breath and his eyes stared like some giant goldfish. Suddenly he vomited. I thought this would be just about the best time to look in the pram. It was, of course, quite empty.

'Unlucky, John,' I panted. 'Good try, though, good try.'

The pram was a decrepit old thing, full of holes. It had been left out for the kids to play with, but, by Christ, he'd thought quickly.

I led him back to the area car and some few minutes later we were in the charge room at Wharf Road. He looked across at me with a weak smile.

'Nearly 'ad yer, though, Ginger, didn't I?'

The Block was always forming action committees, although they never lasted very long. Within a month or so of being formed, they would break up in disarray. Then the more dominating characters would emerge. These would seek media publicity for their rehousing and they would achieve far more than their more orthodox predecessors. Many of these people were classified as hot-heads; extremists; even megalomaniacs. Yet the fact is they got things done. People became aware of Bridewell Dwellings. There's nothing like a TV programme (always inaccurate, of course) for gingering up a council housing committee.

One such character was Susan Avis. Quite frankly, Susan terrified me. In any argument or difference of opinion, she would use reasoned logic for all of fifteen seconds. If that failed, she would attempt to persuade her opponent with whatever was conveniently at hand: her fingernails, chairs, scissors, knives and, for really special debating foes – and that usually included the police – a meat cleaver. She possessed a ferocious, evil temper and looked capable of chewing horseshoes. Yet just occasionally I had seen her look really attractive. She was trim, firm bodied and quite vivacious. She was reputed to be a 'Tom', yet although she had convictions for just about everything else, she had none for prostitution.

Susan's relationships were countless and usually brief. Yet there always seemed to be someone who was prepared to take her on, under her own roof. One of the more lasting of these was a violent young thug some twelve years younger than she. He was slightly more violent and this, perhaps, made for some compatibility; yet it was certainly a long, if bloody relationship.

When he finally left, to serve some years on Dartmoor for a vicious attack on a publican, Susan took up with a surprising new partner. A rather pretty, demure young girl moved in. Susan became even more possessive about her woman than she had been about her man, and fights of jealousy erupted regularly in the nearby pub. Even in public, she had great difficulty in keeping her eyes and her hands from her new lover. When late one night the girl finally ran out on her, Susan went on a drunken binge that lasted for days.

Perhaps the Block gets through to everyone eventually, because Susan finally mellowed. I had to call on her early one evening to give her a date of hearing for a Crown Court trial. I wasn't overthrilled about this, but then any knock on her door would always prove interesting. That day kept up the average. My apprehensive tap was answered by a tall, slim young man. I was quite taken aback. He wore a low-cut, green party frock, high heels and smelt strongly of Estée Lauder.

'Oh, excuse me,' he said casually, 'but I've just climbed out of the bath.'

I gave him the message and heard Susan's voice calling from inside the flat.

'Thank you, officer, thank you.'

Thank you!! I immediately checked to see if I had the right flat. Perhaps she'd had a sex change or was about to die and was trying to go 'good'. It was only when I reached the street level again that I realised Bridewell Dwellings did not possess bathrooms! Oh well, I thought, anything provided it keeps her quiet.

The market that was immediately adjacent to the Bridewell Row was a constant source of revenue for many of the less law-abiding tenants of the Block. Sometimes the pickings would be so good that the culprits would become over-confident, even blasé. One persistent mugger was finally arrested after diligent work by a Wharf Road detective and an identification parade was held. The detective held no great hopes of a positive identification. During the weeks since the theft the suspect had changed his hair-style and grown a beard. To his surprise, however, the woman almost ran straight to the villain and slapped him hard around the face saying: 'That's the bastard!'

'Are you sure?' said the detective, wondering how he

was going to explain away the wallop if she'd got it wrong.

'Am I sure?' she echoed. 'He's still wearing my fucking bracelet.'

Usually, though, any stolen property that found its way into the Block was disposed of very quickly. That is, provided there was sufficient time. A shoe-selling stallholder in the Sunday market kept an enclosed, heavily locked lorry parked in the street, just across from the Bridewell Row playpark. He would return at frequent intervals to replenish the stocks on his stall. He was always most careful to padlock both bars across the heavy rear doors of the vehicle. The market always closes on Sundays a little after 1 p.m. Many traders then tidy up their stock rapidly, in order to have a quick pint before the pubs shut. The shoe-seller left the pub around 2 p.m., having previously returned all of his unsold shoes to his lorry. As he neared his vehicle, he realized the driver's door window was missing. On closer inspection, so was a panel from the rear of the cabin. On even *closer* inspection, so was his stock!

I was driving a brand-new area car that Sunday. Our Wolseley 110s had become obsolete and I was attempting to familiarize myself with a 2.4 Jaguar. It was taking some getting used to. My R/T operator was my old friend Derek Blake and he accepted the call to a theft of 300 pairs of boots and shoes. One did not have to be a super-tec to realize where the shoes had gone. The problem was how best to get them back? It was quite a pleasant sunny afternoon as the three of us walked across the playground towards the Block. I gazed up at the buildings, where several tenants were enjoying the autumn sunshine by sitting at their windows. Perhaps a little bluff might work? After all, those flats had a grapevine that would have shamed witch-doctors.

'Well, there's only one thing for it,' I said loudly to the stallholder. 'We'll have to get a warrant and search all of these flats.' (An impossibility, of course.) 'Let's go back to your lorry and you can make out an inventory.'

We returned to the vehicle and busied ourselves doing nothing for some ten minutes. We then returned to Bridewell Row. An amazing sight met us. There were literally hundreds of boots and shoes scattered all over the roadway! The stallholder at first thought he had found more than he had lost! He drove his lorry round into the Row and we helped him reload. When we had finished, we stood in a group while Derek completed his report. A 'scuffling' noise caused me to look around. There was a snotty-nosed four-year-old kid walking across the park wearing two of the longest ladies' knee-length boots that I had ever seen!

'Come here, you little sod,' exclaimed the trader.

'You leave him alone,' came a yell from an open window. 'I bought them yesterday!'

'Well, you were well had over,' shouted back the trader, ''cos they're odd sizes and different colours!'

Swiftly upending the 'little sod', he reclaimed his last pair of boots and gratefully left for home. Derek and I also drove away, to a general chorus of 'all coppers are bastards'.

A few years later a date was agreed for the demolition of the Block and families finally began to move out. There was no great exodus, just a constant trickle, as council accommodation became available in other parts of the borough. This is always a time of great disruption. As families move out, so scavengers, in the shape of scrap dealers and vandals, move in. Life for those remaining becomes intolerable. It was also about this time that some overdue re-organizing of policing was begun. Before that period, most reported crime was investigated by a CID officer. By the early 1960s with crime figures rising dramatically, this was becoming impossible. All uniform officers were therefore sent on a 'minor crimes' course in an effort to combat this escalation.

I had returned to the station that Monday after my week-long course and dutifully reported to my old friend 'Taff' Thomas, the Minor Crimes Officer. It was his task to allocate the reported crimes.

'What super crime have you got for Wharf Road's ace crime-buster then?' I asked a little acidly.

'Theft,' he announced, as if it were as rare as a thistle in a brassiere. 'Theft of half-a-quid's-worth of groceries. How about that?'

'Well, what are we standing about for?' I demanded. 'I'll alert Interpol, close all ports and turn the Welsh back at the border. I feel my entire career has been aimed at this one big job. If you get me a reliable detective sergeant to assist me with my enquiries, I'll crack this case for you in no time.'

'I shouldn't bother,' he said wearily. 'Panda One doubts if the loser ever had them in the first place. I just feel that someone should go round to see him, that's all.'

'Where is it?'

'Number 1, Bridewell Dwellings.'

'Oh Gawd, I might have known! Name?'

'Robinson.'

I muttered to myself all the way to the Block. What idiot doesn't know if he has lost his groceries? Was this what I joined the force for? Was this my destiny: to track down half a pound of cooking fat, a tin of sardines and a small jar of pickled beetroots, bottled in Poland? Turning into the Row, it was strange to see it so empty. Number 1 appeared to be the only occupied flat in the first entrance.

It is probably totally illogical but I always look at the curtains of any house that I enter as a police officer. Perhaps I feel they reflect the character of the occupier. I don't know; but I do know that my heart sank when I saw these. They were little more than wispy rags. The windows were filthy and the front door had the dirt of months upon it. The remains of a broken milk bottle lay all around the front doorstep. After the third knock, I heard shuffling on the other side of the door. Two bolts were pulled back, locks were turned and the door opened to reveal an elderly gentleman of about ninety years, who peered at me with sightless eyes.

'You will have to speak up because I'm deaf,' was his greeting.

Every other word was punctuated with what appeared to be a fight for breath. I yelled the nature of my enquiry and he eventually led me into the only room in the flat which he used. The weather outside was bitter and the wind was cutting. Inside, the only form of heating was a very small, antiquated one-bar electric fire. It seemed colder in the flat than out in the street. The room contained a bed, narrow and sagging, with an old coat in lieu of an eiderdown. A very cluttered chest of drawers stood in one corner. In the centre of the room a bare wooden table supported a large chipped cup, a torn packet of sugar, a grey-looking loaf, and finally a dirty milk bottle dominated the whole, like a lighthouse in a nightmare surrealist painting. There was one wooden chair, to which he directed me. In front of the fire was a small wooden box and a gas ring. The door of the wall cupboard was slightly ajar and I could see a few stores. The floorboards were bare, and scattered about were the butts of tiny handmade cigarettes which looked as if they had never contained tobacco even in their original rolling.

I looked at the 'loser'. His lifeless eyes always seemed directed six inches or so above my head. His hair was short but very thick and white. His skin was almost transparent with age, while his straight, classical features suggested that he had been a striking-looking man in his youth. His suit was about twenty years old and badly stained, but appeared to have the cut of a good tailor in spite of the ravages of time. He was painfully thin and the knuckles of his bony hands seemed almost to pierce his gossamer-like skin.

I heard a movement behind me. I turned to see the dirty muslin curtain standing out at right angles to the wall; it had been caught by a sudden gust of wind surging through the broken windows. The gust blew itself out and the curtains sagged back into place as if the struggle had been all too much for it.

'I understand you've lost some groceries, Pop!' I shouted.

'Yes. You see, someone has a duplicate key and gets in here every night and takes my food and money.'

'But you have two bolts on the door,' I yelled.

'Yes, I know, but they are very clever.'

'Do you live here on your own?' I bawled.

'Yes.'

'Who comes to see you?'

'Only my son – about every six months or so.'

'How long have you lived here, then?'

'Ten years.'

I was stunned. Ten years! No one to visit him, blind deaf and ninety! In the centre of eight million people. What have we done to this man?

Another gust of wind caused me to turn again. There I saw what looked like 'half-a-quid's-worth' of groceries among the medicine bottles and pills that cluttered the chest of drawers. I did not say anything but quietly put them into his cupboard with the rest of the stores.

'Look, Pop,' I said, 'I'll come and see you again soon.'

'But how about my groceries?' he insisted, staring even harder into the space I had just left.

'I'm going to make some enquiries, that's all. Now don't you worry, I'll be back,' I assured him.

'Please promise you will get my locks changed, please,' he pleaded. 'I'm terrified here at nights.'

'I promise.'

I left him sitting by his dim fire, and as I stepped out into the comparative warmth of the freezing street a peculiar feeling of guilt and relief swept over me. First I contacted the local social services, who were appalled that no one had thought to tell them of his circumstances. Then I went to the council caretaker of a neighbouring estate. Although Bridewell Dwellings was not his responsibility he readily offered to change the locks. We knew, of course, there were no duplicate keys; no mysterious intruder; no nocturnal phantom. Just a very cold and poor, blind and deaf and – above all – lonely old man.

It was my weekly leave the following day, so it was two days before I went to see Mr Robinson again. The doors and windows of his flat were boarded up. The broken bottle still littered the approaches to his front door, but of the occupier there was no sign. I telephoned the social services.

'Yes, we've managed to get the old chap into a home. Life should now be a little better for him.'

Again I experienced the feeling of guilt and relief. After all, hadn't I done my bit? He was safe now, wasn't he? They would look after him.

The following day I again called at the office of the social services.

'Mr Robinson? I'm sorry, he died yesterday.'

I felt crushed this time. No feeling of relief, just monumental guilt. It is true that George Robinson had had a long existence: ninety years is a hell of a time in this world. But must all of the George Robinsons be made to feel that they have outstayed their welcome?

What of his son who let him fade away?

What of his neighbours who seemed indifferent?

And what of me – who did not see him because he was inconsiderate enough to be dying on my leave day?

As I returned to the station, my journey took me past

number 1, Bridewell Dwellings. I stopped for a moment outside the filthy front door. The broken glass bottle seemed like a shattered memorial.

The crime book at Wharf Road carried an entry for Mr Robinson and his groceries: 'Property mislaid by loser, therefore not recorded as a crime.'

Not a crime?

I think it was, and 'the Block' and I were accessories.

Gay Liberation Front

'You have two demonstrations today, gentlemen. The Gay Liberation Front is marching in the morning and an anti-apartheid group is marching in the afternoon. It is going to be a long day, I'm afraid, but it should pass fairly smoothly. The anti-apartheid affair is quite a small one. It will no doubt be noisy but they are well organized so no trouble is really expected.

'Your main task, therefore, is to be the mobile reserve for the Gay Libbers' march. Fifteen hundred protesters of both sexes are marching through the West End. They'll begin at Westminster and terminate near the British Museum in Bloomsbury. Again, no aggravation is expected from the marchers. If there is going to be any trouble at all, it may come from members of the public on the route. Some people do get terribly wound up about a public display by homosexuals. The sight of a large man in a blue frock does tend to get up their backs – if you'll pardon the expression – so pay particular attention to the crowd. Any questions?'

'What are the Gays protesting about?' said a voice from the back.

'Us! They think we don't like 'em. I don't know how any of you feel about them, but to be honest, I am totally indifferent. One thing's for sure, they are usually amongst the most peaceful of protesters, so all in all it should be a quiet, boring day. If there are no more questions then perhaps you will care to board the two transit vans outside the station.'

Inspector Grant finished his briefing and twenty men trooped down the front steps of Wharf Road Police Station and boarded the vehicles. Thirty minutes later, together with two hundred or so other policemen from all over London, we were seated in the canteen at Scotland Yard. Here, a substantial late breakfast was served to each officer, who, having been thoroughly fed and watered, was then considered fit for come-what-may.

The task of a travelling reserve is very simple. The transit van will leap-frog the head of the march and, in ninety per cent of cases, men will only leave the vehicle to stretch their legs or, if it is a warm day, surreptitiously purchase an ice-cream. (For some reason, the sight of a coach load of coppers licking cornets reduces tourists to a babbling, camera flashing frenzy. I think I have been on most state, ceremonial and street disturbances in London over the last twenty-nine years and, like all my colleagues, I must have been photographed hundreds of times. It would be safe to assume that in the vast majority of these pictures, I am licking a cornet. I sometimes have this mental vision of elderly retired people from all corners of the world removing those old holiday snaps from the depths of the drawers and nostalgically reminiscing about the cornet-loving policemen of London. By far the most impressive aspect of these ice-cream purchases is the instant slashing of prices. The swarthy, mustachioed seller, serenely charging a patient line of Japanese £1 per cornet, rapidly drops his price to a more realistic rate when he sees the local constabulary.)

Our transit's first stop was opposite 10 Downing Street. This was my first opportunity to study the marchers in any great detail. Easily the most awe-inspiring part of the procession, apart from its actual size, was the magnificent costumes of some of the men. Many were so ornately splendid, they would have shamed peacocks. Some were dressed as ballerinas, precise in every detail, even down to the shoes. Others promenaded in exquisitely sequined silk trouser-suits. Some, of course, were simply grotesque. In the main, however, elegance triumphed.

The females, on the other hand, were terribly disappointing. Perhaps I was unlucky because I never saw the entire march, but almost every woman that I did see looked like a Japanese Sumo-wrestler. These women operated mainly in jean-clad pairs. The older of the two was usually aged about thirty, short of stature and quite shapeless, obviously scorning any type of support garment. She would, however, be very vociferous, screeching out loudly her chants and slogans. The younger half of this partnership was usually in her late teens, without bra or make-up and extremely plain-looking. She wore the obligatory tee-shirt, displaying on the front such slogans as: 'Don't knock it till you've tried it' and 'Love your brother *AND* your sister'. She would be a little less plump than her 'sister' but accurately echoed her rhetoric in a distinctly shriller tone. The roles of the sexes seemed to have been reversed more in the question of dress than in any other single aspect.

Before more than half of the procession had passed, we received our first call on the transit radio and, reluctantly, we had to leave our excellent vantage point at Downing Street. From there to Parliament Square is barely a quarter of a mile, so within a few moments we had arrived – to scenes of great confusion. Apparently six of the demonstrators had been arrested for some minor offences and the rear half of the procession had stopped in sympathy. Meanwhile the front half, who probably knew nothing about it anyway, had sailed serenely on. The demonstration had only been in progress a few minutes and already we had two separate marches. To fan the flames even further, some of the marchers had decided to sit down in the road. This action immediately lost the sympathy of most passing drivers, who were attempting to negotiate all the other hazards of West End traffic. This was not a good start to the day.

Two older-than-usual policemen had just arrested a young demonstrator. They asked our driver to convey him to Bow Street Police Station, which was being used that day as a charging centre. The young man was wearing a fiercely scarlet silk jacket with large puffy sleeves. His eyes were heavily made up and his bright lipstick glinted in certain angles of light. He said nothing at first but showed his displeasure by a series of plaintive, dramatic hand-gestures, the type that one sees in old-time silent movies.

The only space available for him to sit was between the rear seats and the door. As the youth reluctantly squeezed into this confined space, he reminded me more and more of a captured butterfly.

'I don't fink I should be 'ere at all,' he said in a gentle cockney voice that somehow surprised me.

The two arresting officers, who had managed some alternative and swifter means of transport, were waiting for us at the front of Bow Street Police Station. One of our group opened the rear door of the vehicle and our prisoner almost rolled into the roadway.

'Come on, you,' said one of the captors, a shade too brusquely, I thought, and he was led quickly into the station.

'What was he nicked for?' I asked, almost to myself.

'Offensive weapon,' came an anonymous reply.

'Funny, I didn't think he looked the type. What sort of weapon was it?' I queried.

'Meat cleaver.'

'Meat cleaver! And I thought he looked like a bloody butterfly!'

'You never were a good judge of character,' said my colleague, Lou Peters.

We rejoined the main body of the march and eventually arrived in Malet Street, Bloomsbury, where the marchers were to have a short meeting and then disband. Although several banners denouncing a fairly wide variety of homosexual persecutions were displayed, the mood of the crowd had changed to one that was purely anti-police. I had never before experienced a reaction quite like this. It was truly venomous. It seemed to me that their frustrations with a society which they saw as hostile or indifferent were being worked out directly against the coppers on the route. Until that Saturday I had had great sympathy with their cause. In my mind I now questioned the validity of their organization.

Inspector Grant's radio suddenly crackled into life and he called to us.

'Back to the transit, lads, they're all going to march on Bow Street Police Station, to demonstrate about the arrests that were made in Parliament Square.'

As I climbed up into the door of the transit, I heard a shrill voice cut through the hubbub of the crowd.

'Come out, you homosexual policemen! We know you're there!'

That at least gave me my first smile of the day.

Bow Street Police Station is situated, of course, in Bow Street. Also in that section of street, and directly opposite the station itself, is Covent Garden Opera House. The Wharf Road contingent's task was to throw a cordon across the south end of the street. People could leave, but none could enter. Other serials of police were stationed at the north end of the street with presumably the same instructions. The result of this action was immediately to isolate not just the police station but also the Opera House and a ladies' dress shop which, until that moment, I had never heard of, but which is now engrained on my memory for all time.

The first fact to emerge from any police cordon, no

matter how tightly drawn, is its apparent invisibility to fifty per cent of the public. My position in the line, with two of my colleagues, was on the west footway. Now it would be fair to assume that three policemen, standing in a line across the entire pavement and to all intents and purposes totally blocking it, would have some sort of significance. Especially when the line consisted of some twenty coppers, two sergeants and an inspector, and continued across the road and up to the wall on the opposite pavement. But no. At least half of the pedestrians that approach the line will turn sideways on, in an effort to squeeze through. The following conversation will usually take place.

Policeman: 'Er – excuse me, guv [or madam], you can't come through here.'
Guv(or madam): 'Oh! Can't I?'
Policeman: 'No.'
Guv (or madam) thinks for a while, then says in a puzzled voice: 'Oh, why is that, is the Queen coming?'
Policeman: 'Yes, about fifteen hundred of 'em, and they're advancing on Bow Street Police Station.'
Guv (or madam): 'Oh, I see' – pauses for a moment and then adds – 'but I have to get through!'
Policeman: 'Sorry, you can't.'
Guv (or madam): 'Oh, but I've parked my car in [any nearby sidestreet] and I want to go home.'
Policeman: 'Then simply walk around the block and into the next street.'
Guv (or madam): 'Oh! Can I do that, then?'
Policeman: 'Yes.'
Guv (or madam): 'Oh, thanks' – turns to walk away, pauses, then adds as an afterthought – 'Why are all you policemen here?'

That is a conversation which, with slight local

alterations, will take place on any police cordon anywhere in London. In Bow Street on a summer Saturday afternoon, however, one has the additional entertainment of the aforementioned Opera House *and* Laura Ashley's dress shop. The big problem for the opera lovers was that all telephone bookings had to be paid for and collected by 4 p.m. for that day's performance. On the other hand, since the street was closed, then the chances of their being sold to anyone else were fairly remote. Opera lovers seemed to understand and accept this. *Not* so the frock-shop people, however.

Laura Ashley's! I just cannot think why I had never heard of the shop before. I am now convinced that every female in London on a Saturday afternoon is making for the damn place and, above all, determined to get there!

After about thirty minutes I lost count of the number of times I had said, 'You can't go through because fifteen hundred homosexuals . . . etc. etc.'

'Oh, I only want to go to Laura Ashley's!'

After forty-five minutes my voice went. I decided to write a brief explanation of exactly why the road was closed. I scribbled it down on a page of a notebook that I always carry, and attached the small page to my whistle chain on the front of my jacket. It read as follows:

> This road is closed because 1500 homosexuals are advancing on Bow Street – the north end. [I didn't know if that location was strictly true, but as we were at the south end and all seemed fairly quiet, there seemed little point in unnecessarily alarming the middle-classes.] All access is restricted. Covent Garden opera tickets are being held until the cordon is lifted. [Another blatant guess on my part.] *No!* You cannot go to Laura Ashley's!

Within a space of three minutes, a queue had formed to

read this notice. Japanese tourists, their fingers pointing at it, posed smilingly beside it, not, of course, being able to understand a word of it. Every other reader seemed to frown deeply and say, 'Oh! We cannot go to Laura Ashley's, then? I wonder why that is?' The notice at least had the effect of getting them to talk among themselves, blessedly ignoring me.

After about ten minutes I was approached by Inspector Grant.

'You can't stand there with a bloody notice pinned to your chest. You look like bloody Guy Fawkes. Take it off!'

'Well I'm fed up telling people why they can't walk up this sodding street. Besides, they never believe me the first time I tell them and I always have to repeat it. Anyway, I'm losing my voice.'

'Well, pin it on to the wall if you like, but you can't keep it on your whistle chain,' he said, in a slow tone that he usually reserved for admonishing four-year-olds.

After a brief search of my pockets, I discovered an old pencil stub, which I used to secure the notice to the rough brick wall.

If I had been surprised at the effect the thing had had when attached to my chest, I was astounded by what happened when I attached it to the wall. The orderly queue at my whistle chain dissolved into a milling throng, pushing and jostling in an effort to read the note. It reminded me of the execution notices that used to be pinned to the doors of prisons after a hanging. The only difference was probably in the readers' dialogue. Instead of 'God rest his soul', one would hear: 'But I simply must change this dress.'

The group of people attempting to read the notice in itself formed a barrier to any access along the Bow Street pavement. I therefore moved from the wall to the kerbside, simply to avoid the jostling of the crowd. It was at this moment that my attention was drawn to a tall, stunningly attractive sun-tanned woman. She was very smartly dressed and in her late thirties.

'Excuse me, officer.' (The few words immediately gave her away as an obvious Australian.) 'D'yer mind telling me what the hell's going on here?'

I said nothing but pointed to the notice. She looked puzzled but duly joined the group. She towered over several Asiatics who had by this time gradually eased their way to the front.

'All back on the transit, lads! We're dismissed!'

The blessed words that every copper who has just spent four hours standing on alternate legs loves to hear. The quiet cordon immediately became a chattering mass as we made our way across the road towards our transit.

'Officer!' came the Australian lady's urgent call.

I paused, not sure whether at this late stage it would be wise to acknowledge.

'Officer!' she repeated.

My curiosity, as always, got the better of me. I turned towards her. She had removed the notice from the wall and was studying it intently. I decided on impulse to rescue the thing (in fact, I still have it), and returned to my former position on the pavement.

'The road's open now, luv, you can go through,' I explained as I took the notice from her well-manicured hand.

'Officer,' she said in a much quieter tone, 'Officer, can I ask you a question?'

'Yes – but make it quick. I'm supposed to be in that transit,' I said a little sharply.

'Who the fuck's Laura Ashley?'

I looked at her for a few seconds in total amazement. Then, laughing almost uncontrollably, I placed my hands on either side of her face.

'Oh, I love you! Where've you been all day? I've been looking for you all afternoon!'

I turned and ran quickly across the road to the now throbbing transit.

'Officer! Officer!'

I quickly glanced back as I climbed the vehicle steps.

'Who – is – she?' she silently mouthed. Her face then broke into a huge smile and she waved cheerily.

Still shaking my head, I took my seat in the transit next to Lou Peters.

'That's a great-looking bird you've just been talking to,' he said enviously.

'She's not just good-looking – she's bloody unique!' I answered happily.

Section-house

When the changes of the 1960s dragged the Metropolitan Police reluctantly into the twentieth century, one of the last bastions to fall was the single men's section-house. These institutions were usually built over the station itself, or very nearby. This proximity was never intended as a convenience for the residents. It was purely a means of ensuring a great number of additional policemen at a moment's notice. The section-houses were nineteenth-century in design and application. Life in them was both intimate and barbaric.

The usual design closely resembled a long barrack-room. The bed spaces, referred to as 'bunks', were partitioned off by seven-foot plywood screens which were raised twelve inches from the floor. There was just enough room for a hard single bed and a heavy, chest-high, wooden locker. A small shelf protruded from high up on the back wall, and a couple of hooks, which sufficed as a wardrobe, hung down.

Ablutions could be performed in the eight or so hand basins set into a long slab of grey marble. In addition there were a couple of WCs, three showers and two enormous white enamelled baths. These baths were so large that smaller residents had been known to pin up the following notice:

Shallow end ——— Deep end

In the larger section-houses – those with say, forty or more beds – and in those adjacent to the local police station, for at least part of the day a canteen would be provided. The obvious problem with this amenity was that policemen, like all shift workers, do not eat at civilized times. Catering, therefore, became something of a problem. Section-houses were generally considered the greatest incentive to marriage since the invention of the shotgun. Most men's ideal would have been a good-looking local girl who could cook. Sometimes a man would be really lucky and find not just an attractive girl but one with a mother who could also cook. This would be bliss indeed. Unfortunately, this sort of relationship was rare. In the main, life for the single man was very much a compromise. For many it rested with a simple dilemma: you could kiss it, or you could eat it – but you couldn't have both!

Each section-house was provided with a kitchen containing a huge grimy gas-stove where men were expected to do their own cooking. Next door would be the mess-room where the inhabitants valiantly attempted to eat the swamp-like creations they had prepared – always, of course, from a frying pan. A rough rule of thumb in any section-house would be: 'If you can fry it, you can eat it.' By rights, these frying pans should now all hang in industrial museums. They were huge, shallow containers that looked as if they belonged underneath the leaking sumps of omnibuses. Food that had been cooked in them frequently bore out this theory.

In addition to these tribulations, Wharf Road section-house had another – the Blackfriars to Croydon railway line which ran immediately beneath its windows.

As a result of this fascinating environment, these buildings evolved their own breed of men. There are, arguably, a greater number of different characters to be found in a police section-house than in any other comparable establishment. There are many reasons for this, the main one being that the police force itself is a great melting pot. All sorts of characters, misfits and eccentrics gravitate to it. All the section-house does is to assemble them under one roof. Ben Huxley, for instance, was one of nature's gentle people, quiet, placid and unruffled . . . except during shunting time on the railway line that ran directly under his window. On these occasions his twenty-minute slanging matches with the engine driver, usually around three in the morning, would be one of the features of the week.

Brian Smiley, who lived on the second floor, was also your strong, silent type. This tall, non-smoking, non-drinking, non-talking zombie would turn everyone's stomach in the mess-room, simply by placing shredded wheat on every meal he ate. Those 'strands of real wheat' would cascade down everything from salads to stews.

My personal favourite was Slim Parker, a portly twenty-six-year-old West Countryman with a large red face and a real Cornish 'burr'. He was into classical music in a very big way. Each year he would hitch-hike to La Scala, Milan, for his holiday. He would also fall in love on average twice monthly – nearly always with ladies of somewhat doubtful repute.

Most of the noise that manifested itself in the section-house would take place in the mess-room. Cards, conversations, records, radios, arguments and the consumption of a whole range of appallingly cooked meals would be taking place or playing at any one time throughout the day. In the midst of this nightmare of sound would be Slim. He would be sitting with his ear glued to his elderly pre-war radio, playing its seemingly elderly pre-war music. Unknown string quartets, scratching out some tuneless medieval fugue, would be food and drink to Slim. At these moments he was oblivious to the world.

Slim's one great disappointment was the absence of anyone to share his love of music. The girls he usually met would have had great difficulty in recognizing a mouth organ, therefore Slim really had to go it alone. Then, one day in the Duke of Sutherland, he thought his luck had changed. Slim happened to mention his love of serious music to a girl at the bar. To his utter delight, his new friend said she also adored the classics. Slim required very little encouragement in a situation like this and was soon in the throes of a great oration on his favourite composer – Wagner. Around this period, the powerful Norwegian Wagnerian singer, Kirsten Flagstad, was at her peak.

'What do you think of Kirsten Flagstad?' asked Slim, with burning curiosity.

The girl thought hard for a while and then replied, 'I'm not sure I've ever heard it – how does it go?'

Slim knew a great deal about music, but he didn't know a thing about women. One day he ran away with Maud, a local bar-maid, and we never saw him again. Maud was never a music-lover although, to be fair, she was married to the pub's pianist; and for Slim – that was close.

Our two main performers in Wharf Road, however, were Reg and Bill, who were as different as chalk and cheese but politely tolerated each other.

Reg was the station bookmaker and owned a one-sixteenth share in a greyhound. He knew the family history and running form of every horse, dog and jockey in any race anywhere in the country. He was courting a very attractive local girl, if 'courting' was the correct word. For thirteen years Reg had been engaged to Sheila and his feet were firmly under the family table – to such an extent that the spectacles he wore in times of stress (he would never admit to needing glasses normally) were a pair that he had bought from Sheila's Mum, for five shillings.

By virtue of his length of service, Reg was the uncrowned king of a section-house where seniority counted for a great deal. An example of this was Reg's traditional right to one of the two fireside armchairs, which were always the prerogative of the two longest serving inmates. They were also to be Reg's ultimate undoing. While enjoying an afternoon nap, he adopted such a position that he injured his neck. The damage was so severe that he was subsequently discharged from the force on medical grounds.

There are many problems in trying to sleep above a busy police station. The screaming sirens, roaring engines, reluctant prisoners and singing drunks all conspire to demolish the tranquillity so eagerly sought by a weary copper. Yet distressing though these noises may be, they do not compare with the sleep-shattering sound of a yapping dog. Tether any dog in a police station yard and immediately it is seized by an uncontrollable desire to yap. It never barks, it always yaps. The smaller the dog, the greater the yap. To be fair, often the dog is simply complaining about his illegal incarceration. Many a scruffy mongrel has been dragged protesting from his own doorstep by some interfering, canine-loving idiot who is convinced he has found yet another unhappy lost dog.

Nothing would throw Reg's sleep-mechanism into disarray faster than a noisy dog. Trains would rattle by, radios would blare, hoovers would hum and Reg would remain as immobile as the Sphinx. But, let the smallest of dogs emit the tiniest of yaps and Reg would emerge through seven layers of sleep quicker than if his feet had been on fire.

At the first sign of a yap Reg would arise like some long-dead mummy in a cheap horror film and search for the keen-bladed knife he always kept by his pillow. Throwing his egg-stained dressing-gown around his large shoulders, he would begin his descent from the second floor and into the station yard. Possibly the most alarming sight that any recruit could ever experience was to be suddenly confronted by this madman staggering down the staircase in his trance-like state, his hair hanging down and the knife glinting in his hand.

He would totter across the cobbled yard to the kennels, where he could never actually see the animal. The reason for this was that no dog in creation wished to do anything other than hide when the muttering Reg advanced upon him with a knife.

He need not have feared, however; Reg, when eventually he found the dog, would simply cut its string and within seconds the grateful cur would leg it out of the back gate, quicker than a hound out of hell. The entry in the 'Dog Book' next day would show what it always showed when Reg was on night-duty: 'Dog escaped whilst in police custody.'

Bill, on the other hand, was a rapier to Reg's bludgeon. He would rarely be in the building at all. He was a tall smart man who had a great number of interests outside the police force. Not the least of these were women, preferably married. Strictly speaking, no officer was allowed to sleep a night outside the section-house unless he entered his name in the 'Nights Out' book kept in the front office. The errant officer had to state where, and with whom, he could be found. Whereas Reg's relationship with Sheila was nothing if not long-standing, Bill's relationships with his women were invariably of a three-day duration. Therefore, Bill's name figured prominently in the 'Nights Out' book – always at a different address.

Bill relied exclusively, and very successfully, on his undoubted charm. He was a shrewd gambler who took only calculated risks. His interest in horses and dogs did not match Reg's. He preferred to bet on more individual subjects such as his own judgement, or his unquestioned skill at snooker, table-tennis and, above all, cards. At cards he could be positively lethal: he never forgot any card that had been played. Yet most of his success came from his greatest gift of all, the one of 'chat'. Bill was running chat-shows before TV had ever thought of the word. Every card game that Bill ever played was a 'chat-show'. One of his favourite tricks was to play a hand of cards with half of them face up on the table – and still win! He would accomplish this by baffling his opponent with the incessant talk.

Where Bill's charm came into operation best was, strangely enough, at listening. At cards his opponent would simply never be able to slip a word in edgeways, but if anyone was ever prepared to converse on a serious subject, then Bill would listen and absorb. Bill revelled in the thrust and counter-thrust of police discipline. He drove a bus through just about every discipline regulation the force ever drafted, and he did it with the calm satisfaction of an accomplished master.

Just occasionally, even Bill would spend a night in. He would probably not return to the section-house until midnight at the earliest and he would usually be accompanied by a different woman. Bill was never interested in girls – only women, smartly dressed women at that. Now for your average section-house resident, here would be a problem of unprecedented magnitude. Having sufficiently charmed a young woman into actually entering the building, how does one smuggle her up the stairs of an establishment that is exclusively masculine, privacy virtually non-existent?

Bill's answer was simple. Straight through the front door. He would gallantly escort her up the same steps that Reg would later stagger down. He did it with the same panache that he might have used in the ballroom at Claridge's. What's more, this system never once failed him. The only sensible precaution Bill took was never to use his own bunk for his nocturnal activities. He kept a mental note of everyone who was legitimately absent, either sick or on leave. Many a bewildered copper has returned to his bunk after a spell in the Nursing Home, to find all of the hall-marks of a muffled explosion.

The provision of a bed was not, of course, the only problem. In an open-plan establishment, designed exclusively for males, nobody worried too much about modesty, particularly once the cleaners had gone home. Many a sleepy-eyed policeman clad only in his socks has entered the wash-room for an early morning shave and there found, much to his astonishment, a mature, statuesque woman wearing one of Bill's old police shirts, just leaving the toilet. The peak of these erotic adventures came when the same system was used by an enterprising protégé of Bill's. An innocent late-night reveller, seeking to brush his teeth before turning in, discovered two large naked blondes under the showers. Bill's, of course, was the older one.

With the easing of restrictions in the 1960s, Bill bought himself a flat and thereby promptly deprived the rest of the station of enough material to launch six Sunday newspapers. It was also around this period that poor Reg was discharged from the force, and somehow the character of the old section-house was never the same.

Some things did linger for a while. Section-house doctors, for example. Because of the monotony of the frying pan, single policemen suffered more than most from minor stomach ailments – or 'section-house rot', as it was usually called. According to the discipline code, you were either fit or you were unfit. If you were unfit, then you were required to produce a certificate. Because of this situation, some of the old section-house doctors were perhaps more tolerant of the smaller ailments than they might otherwise have been. The Wharf Road GP was a Dr Hatton. He had run a local practice since the 1920s and was readily sympathetic to 'section-house rot'. He also had a most unusual cure: 'Take a week off, lad – go racing!'

While this treatment would work to a degree, it did present problems when one had a genuine illness. The grandstand at Sandown Park, for instance, loses its magic when one has severe gastroenteritis. This was never more apparent than when young Bob Huggins, with just a few months' service in the force, began to feel quite ill. His face, neck and body became red, his temperature rose dramatically to 104° and he had a severe headache.

Bob somehow reached the surgery, and was the last patient of the morning.

''Morning, young man,' said Hatton, 'how are you?'

Bob told him exactly how he was.

'Food poisoning,' said the benevolent doctor after a cursory glance. 'Not surprised in that place! Here's a certificate for a week: have a couple of days in bed, then go racing.'

Clutching his certificate and his prescription, Bob returned to Wharf Road and reported sick. Somehow managing to struggle to the bus-stop, he eventually reached his home at Beckenham.

'Whatever's the matter with you?' said his anxious mother, as Bob collapsed on to the settee.

'Food poisoning,' he gasped.

'Food poisoning? You haven't got food poisoning, you've got chicken pox, any fool can see that!'

Forthwith, she rang for a taxi and mother and son arrived at Dr Hatton's surgery in time for his evening session.

''Evening, young man, how are you?'

'He's got chicken pox!' snapped Bob's mother, instantly on the attack.

'You're right,' said Hatton cheerfully.

'Well, you've put food poisoning on his certificate.'

'Did I?' said the surprised doctor, craning forward for a better view of the ailing Bob. 'Show me.'

Bob slid the certificate weakly across the cluttered table.

After a quick scrawl the certificate was slid quickly back.

'You'll be all right in a couple of days. You can go to Epsom on Thursday.'

Bob glanced wearily down at the form now in his sweating hand. It read: 'Food poisoning *and* chicken pox'.

The waves made by the new section-house seemed to wash away venerable old gentlemen like Dr Hatton. Busy young GPs in group practice no longer recommend a couple of days at Epsom Spring Meeting as a cure for everything except fits. It's a bit sad, really.

Nowadays the whole concept of section-house life has changed. The characters, of course, haven't. The Bills and Regs have long been replaced by the Nigels and Damiens. The names may be different but they are really the same people. The few eccentrics who sent the rest of the residents mad, still do. Except that nowadays it is done much more sophisticatedly. Imagine the horror of a sleeping inhabitant who was rudely awakened by a mouse scuffling across his face and down his bedclothes. He was several floors up in a new section-house building. There was no way that mice could have gnawed and tunnelled their way up seventy feet of walls, insulations and ceilings so soon after completion. This assumption was in fact quite right. The mouse had gained access via the trouser pocket of his room neighbour. It had been fetched up to the sixth floor as food for that person's pet python – and it had escaped!

I bet Reg wouldn't have minded in the least; after all, pythons don't yap.

Women Police

Our gloomy, bug-infested, two-roomed flat in the grey-bricked Victorian tenement, appropriately faced on to a long-established family undertaking business. Alfred Smithers, the proprietor, was a greatly respected local figure. He was a tall lean man with a slight stoop. His Maker had seen fit to cast him in the literary image of all undertakers. His skin was stretched taut across his face and his eyes had retreated into two deep sockets, like moles evading the light.

When Alf spared one of his rare thin smiles, his large yellowing teeth emphasized the straight crack across the front of his face. Yet with just the occasional exception, Alf was a kindly, if sanctimonious man. He had the ability to speak to all the local adults authoritatively and with sufficient detachment to preserve an air of awe and reverence.

If Alf was 'detached' with adults, then he was totally oblivious to kids. Undertakers, even in those mid-1930s, would expect very little business from eight- and nine-year-olds. Better by far to save the civilities for their parents or even more profitably, grandparents.

Because of the mystery and folk-lore that surrounded most of his trade, he suffered little at the hands of mischievous children. Usually they would hurry past his shop with their caps pulled over their eyes and their heads down. If the yard gates were opened, the sound of drilling and banging could usually be heard, coming from the workshop. We all knew what this meant: yet another body was being screwed down into its final position. Long screws, eighteen inches in length, went through the body and into the casket. This was to prevent the dead person from sitting upright and terrifying mourners. We were very privileged to know this information; it was really a trade secret and had only been discovered because Billy Simpson had an uncle who worked in the local mortuary. Billy Simpson therefore was the street authority on all matters relating to the dead.

There was, however, one aspect of 'Alfred Smithers Funeral Director' that did attract us kids. In the window, proudly displayed next to a marble flower vase (in itself a 'Unique Alfred Smithers Accessory'), were the photographs of three local funerals that had been *real* occasions.

First was Jock Brindles. Jock had kept the betting pitch in the alley at the rear of the King's Arms. That funeral had been a really splendid turn-out. Jock's wife and two daughters had worn *real* fur coats and nearly all of the accompanying ladies had worn, at the very least, a fox stole. Several of Jock's bookmaking rivals had turned out in their best fawn Crombie overcoats and it was even rumoured that the mourners were afterwards treated to salmon and cucumber sandwiches for tea!

The second photograph was of the funeral of old George Wilkinson, the licensee of the King's Arms. Many of the fox stoles that were exhibited in Jock Brindles's photograph could be clearly seen around different necks in old George's picture.

The third picture was of the funeral of some high-ranking local police officer. It was obvious that the whole of the personnel of Stone's End Police Station had taken part in the procession that followed the cortège. Among the hundred or so great-coated, big-bellied, heavily booted policemen was *one* solitary female. She wore a long shapeless jacket, a long shapeless skirt, an enormous navy-blue pith-helmet and a pair of huge lace-up boots.

When I look back on those distant childhood memories, I somehow imagine her sporting a moustache and an athletic support. Somewhere, I feel, under that pile of bullet-proof navy-blue serge was most certainly a woman – but it would have taken a very persevering man to have confirmed it. Yet women these policewomen were, and very courageous women at that. They had first been recruited into the police during the war of some twenty years before and little had changed for them since that time, neither in dress, attitudes nor job. That was how it was to remain for almost another twenty-five years. Their uniform, of course, did change; by the 1950s it had become quite smart. Basically, though, a woman police constable's role at any station, certainly up until the mid-seventies, would be almost exclusively with women and young children and with the exception of the occasional observation or raid, little else besides. There were, of course, notable exceptions to this rule, the classic one being WPC Ethel Bush, who in 1956 was awarded the George Medal for her bravery in acting as a decoy to trap a violent rapist. The blows he rained on her head with a bar of iron nearly ended her life.

Of all the comprehensive changes that have taken place in the force within the last decade, female integration has undoubtedly been the greatest. It has not only opened the door to vast numbers of women but it has taken a very conservative, reluctant-to-change body like the Metropolitan Police and stood it absolutely on its head. Supervising officers of even ten years ago would shake their heads in disbelief if they came back now. Old pre-war guv'nors must be turning in their graves.

It was some time, of course, before the girls were fully accepted by their male counterparts. In fact many older policemen have never accepted them at all. They consider this aspect of the force's development to be a retrograde step. It was only a few years ago that old George, a sixteen-stone copper who looked like an unmade bed, sat enthroned in the only station armchair. Now there's a trim young girl about the size of one of George's legs, sitting in his place. That is quite a revolution. (Not that we do not have our share of *female* sixteen-stone unmade beds.)

A younger man, on the other hand, probably joined with several females in his class at training school and so his whole police career has been geared to them. He therefore finds it not just easy to accept the girls but perfectly normal that they should be there in the first place. Somewhere in the middle of these two views are coppers like myself. Our group has just about overcome our inbuilt male prejudices. The fact is that young girls are carrying out a job of work that for years we said could only be accomplished by a male. Although I now fully accept this, I still marvel at the novelty. To hear a call from the station on the personal radio:

'Anyone take a disturbance in a Walworth Road café?' and then to hear a quiet female reply:

'Yes, give location, I'll go,' still causes me to shake my head in admiration.

For the first twenty years of my service, Wharf Road Station had no more than three WPCs at any one time, usually there were only two. This was in ratio to about ninety men. Since the integration of the force in the mid-seventies their numbers have increased dramatically. Prior to this period, the girls were paid at a lower rate and many aspects of the force were not open to them. They had accomplished this truly marvellous rapport with children and young people – which has never been adequately regained – but, in the main, they did no street duty or patrolling. Now under the new changes, nearly any task or office which was open to a man could also be undertaken by a woman. This meant not just equal pay but equal work. Panda driving; night-duty beats; traffic-points; demonstrations; football crowds. Some women did not care for these changes and left the force. Many others relished the increase in their opportunities and the numbers of WPCs soared tenfold. Many different types of girls began to join, for a whole variety of reasons. Although many of these reasons were the same as the men's, there were also some additions – divorce, for example. Many women, after a disastrous early marriage, were looking for an opportunity to rebuild their lives. Provided there were no children, the police force fulfilled just that need. Some even managed this new life with children – but God knows how they handled that!

As their numbers increased, so they began to evolve a whole new image. This was first noticeable in the newspaper cartoons of the day. Prior to the seventies, a policewoman had always been drawn to look like someone's mother-in-law. Now she looked like their daughter. Like daughters, they appear vulnerable and unprotected. They do not, for example, carry a truncheon, neither do they wear protective headgear. In the first instance they have absolutely nowhere to carry the truncheon and, in the second, no satisfactory method of head protection for girls has yet been issued. Their own ingenuity has to compensate for this vulnerability. Their handbags are, however, a source of great fascination. Whereas the average male copper scatters his duty requirements all over his uniform – in jacket pockets, trouser pockets, shirts etc., the girls carry theirs in their handbag. The amount of junk they have in these bags is truly incredible. I have seen scrapyards with less.

While their material armaments may be nil, they are very well equipped with their own degree of female cunning. This they use to good effect. A specialist in this field is Jenny who works with me in my job as a community copper. One autumn morning she was posted outside the Labour Party Headquarters in Walworth Road. Inside, the Party was holding a meeting prior to its turbulent 1980

Blackpool conference. Now we have very little in the way of important buildings, structures, sports grounds or celebrated homes on the Wharf Road manor. Those we do have, we tend to fuss over. The Labour Party Headquarters is really our only claim to fame. Jenny was not only posted outside the place but given strict instructions not to leave it.

After about an hour, her attention was drawn to an elderly blind lady, waiting with an escort to cross the road, a little way down from the headquarters. Deciding that Messrs Callaghan, Benn, Healey and Foot would not really mind if she left her point to assist an elderly blind lady across a busy thoroughfare, she hastened away. Stopping the traffic, she called to the lady and her escort. Soon the couple began to cross but when they reached Jenny, who was by now in the middle of the road, the escort nobly handed over his charge to her saying: ''Ere y'are, luv. She's nothing to do with me, I was only 'elping 'er across the road.'

On returning to the footway, Jenny asked the lady in which direction she wished to go. Giving no verbal reply, the old lady opened her large handbag and removed from it a cardboard notice. Printed thereon were the words: 'This lady is foreign. She does not speak English. Will you please place her on a number 12 bus?'

Jenny's instructions had been explicit. 'Under no circumstances are you to leave the premises.' What then should she do with a lady who was, to all intents and purposes, not only deaf, dumb and blind but desirous of securing particular access to a number 12 bus?

'What on earth did you do?' I asked naïvely, uncomfortably aware that I would have been totally bemused.

'I stepped back into the road and stopped a passing number 184 bus. I placed her on the platform and told the conductor to put her off when he saw a number 12. He wasn't all that pleased,' she added, needlessly.

'No! I bet he wasn't!' I replied, instinctively closing my eyes.

I honestly don't think that a man would ever have thought of that solution. I know for sure that I wouldn't have. But there are times when women can be much more aware than men; they can sometimes have a feel for a situation in a way that men rarely have. In addition, of course, they have a greater support from the public than we do. In fact it would not be untrue to say that on some occasions they even have support from the criminals. An ability to deal with such men in situations that may become slightly abrasive can be one of their strong points. Jenny, who is pretty and petite, thuds on to the scales at an intimidating 7 stone 12 lbs. Unassisted, she stopped a belligerent male driver, switched off his ignition, then arrested him for drunken driving. It then took five minutes for four of her male colleagues to get him into a police van. It may well be that he would not have climbed aboard the police van even for her – but she had at least persuaded him to stop in the first place!

Although Jenny is now twenty-one years of age, there are occasions when she looks all of fifteen. This doubtless helps the little-girl-lost image. This in turn can be a useful weapon for any shrewd miss, police girl or otherwise. I realize, of course, that she is much more professional than she sometimes appears. However, during a dawn raid on a Kennington block of flats, into which scores of squatters had allegedly barricaded themselves, she was one of the first officers to enter the building. The following day in the newspapers, she was quite impressed to discover that she was one of a 'force of 200 trained riot police specially prepared for the occasion'.

'I didn't know that you were "specially prepared",' I said. 'What were these special preparations all about?'

'I had a cup of tea and a bacon sandwich,' she answered sweetly.

'And that was all?'
'Well, I did put on some extra clothing.'
'What was that?'
'My Winnie the Pooh tee-shirt, over me bra!'

The workload of police is now many times greater and the pitfalls are far more numerous than even a few years ago. Yet that slightly built girl, who looks about fifteen years old and says things like, 'Can I work inside today, sergeant? I've just had my hair done,' is in reality doing far more genuine police work than many of her male predecessors of a generation ago.

One of the main reasons for this is the introduction of the personal radio plus the escalation of crime and other police commitments. Twenty years ago, it would be by no means unusual for a beat duty man to work several days before he had to deal with a call of any description. He and his uniform would be simply showing the flag. Today an officer can have calls lining up to be dealt with. The 'back-up' for today's policeman may be greater but his volume of face-to-face work in the streets has increased enormously. When a girl patrols the streets, be it on foot or in a panda car, she is expected to cope. Allowances are no doubt instinctively and unofficially made; nevertheless, the job is about the streets – and the streets are not choosy.

This is not to say, of course, that there is now no difference between the sexes. The girls may drive the panda cars, wheel in drunks and roll their own fags, but there is still, to my mind, one fundamental difference (well, all right, two) between us. Call it a prejudice if you want but it is one that is confirmed to me over and over again: women have no sense of direction, they can rarely tell their left from their right. It is in this lack of any sense of direction that WPCs, in my experience, excel.

Bernadette perfectly illustrated this point. A call on her

personal radio asked her for her location. A long silence ensued. Again a request for her location; this time the request was a trifle more insistent.

'Er – I'll have to walk to the end of the street to read the name,' answered Bernie, obviously playing for time.

Yet another long pause, followed in turn by yet another request for a location. Three minutes later came the reply.

'Sumner Road.'

'Sumner Road! What on earth are you doing there?' asked the puzzled station operator.

'Well, I'm er, er, well, I'm lost,' said Bernadette defeated. This was not surprising, considering that she was at least two miles from her patrol and practically in Peckham.

The next day a passing motorist, who should have known better, asked her the way to Brighton. Knowing her own limitations, she came up on the personal radio.

'Can anyone tell me the way to Brighton?'

There was an immediate rush by all the station wits to get in on the act.

'For Christ's sake stay where you are – we only go as far as Camberwell Green!'

Now Bernie is charming and intelligent in every way and she may well go far, but when she arrives there, she may have great difficulty in knowing where the hell she is.

There is, of course, a tight-rope for girls to walk. It is the easiest thing in the world for them to lose their femininity. After a month of working at a station like Wharf Road, young girls and boys will have seen and heard things that they would never encounter in a lifetime in a more sheltered occupation. The trick for both sexes is to be able to absorb all of these experiences, yet not let it corrupt their own thinking or vocabulary. Some find this very difficult. We have had kids who look like trainee nuns, swearing like five-star navvies inside a month. I still wince to hear a fresh-faced girl utter four-letter words needlessly.

I have forever engraved on my memory the first remark I ever heard from one young Cornish lass. She looked so sweet and angelic, she could have done Salvation Army commercials. She entered the canteen with a serene air but apparently not looking her usual country-maid self.

'Heavy night last night, Sarah?' asked a male colleague with mild interest.

'Shut up, you shit – or I'll part your teeth,' replied our sweet Cornish pixie.

Another problem for young girls is the immaturity of some young men (some older ones too, for that matter). On one demonstration I sat on a police coach for what seemed like ages, listening to a foul-mouthed copper talking to his equally thick friend. The whole point of the conversation seemed to be to embarrass the WPC sitting on the seat in front of them. She was able to withstand this verbal sewerage much better than I. Eventually I remonstrated with this oaf and apologized to the girl. 'It's all right,' he said astonishingly, 'she's one of the boys.'

In the first place, with the excellently rounded figure that she possessed, the last thing in the world she looked like was a boy! In the second place, she had no desire to be 'a boy'. And thirdly, why is 'a boy' always supposed to be gutter-minded?

An additional burden for the women has been the leg-pulling that is universal throughout the force. Easily the most popular WPCs are those who can ride a ribbing. A whole new dimension was opened up in this field when integration first began. Some of these teases were thinly disguised defence mechanisms from men who could not come to grips with the changes that were taking place. After all, a man can perform some tasks and his actions will be readily accepted. Yet let a woman attempt the same task and sometimes an entirely different valuation is placed upon her efforts. Two examples clearly illustrate this point.

A young male officer was called to a middle-aged woman who appeared to be suffering from some form of asphyxia. His first and obvious priority was to get her breathing again. He tried both the kiss of life and heart massage but without success. On her arrival at hospital she was pronounced dead. It was the sort of situation that policemen accept as part of their everyday work, and hardly worth mentioning. Yet two months later, Bernadette and Janet became faced with an identical situation, this time with a male sufferer. On this occasion the story spread like wildfire.

In response to a call from a shopkeeper, the girls found a man lying on the floor of a store, apparently breathing his last. Now the names 'Bernadette and Janet' may sound as if these two young ladies have stepped out of a reading book in a primary school. In reality, Bernie's legs go up somewhere near her shoulder blades and Janet is quite simply – a dish.

'I'll give him the "kiss of life" and you massage his heart!' said Janet.

Two excellent, tried-and-tested first-aid measures, no doubt. Sadly the patient died. When the unfortunate woman died some two months before, everyone accepted the cause as asphyxia. There was simply no way, however, that this man would be certified as dying of the same cause. 'Excitement!' was the general opinion. With the lovely Janet's mouth closed over his, and Bernie removing his shirt and rubbing his chest, it was generally accepted that he was the happiest bloke ever to approach St Peter.

'Burke and Hare' were two of the names that were bandied about in the canteen the following day. 'Every time they see a good-looking guy, Janet gives him a passionate kiss and Bernie rips his clothes off,' was one of the kindest stories. Several fellows complained of chest pains (well I certainly did) whenever the two appeared. Fortunately Janet can take a joke and Bernadette spends half her life laughing at herself. Nevertheless, 'Burke and Hare' they remained for some months after.

What appeals to me most about the girls is their ability to do what was traditionally considered a masculine occupation, in a purely feminine way. I find this the most fascinating aspect of the whole task of woman-policing. In short, I suppose, I like to see woman doing a job just like a woman and not a pseudo male.

Joanna had decided that a motorist had committed a traffic-light offence, so she was about to summons him. She searched her pockets but could not find a pen.

'I know I've got one somewhere,' she said to the agitated driver, not fully understanding that it wasn't really the most urgent thing in his life that she should find her pen.

Five minutes later, with the entire contents of her handbag strewn over the bonnet of his car, she acknowledged defeat. Sweeping her arms across the bonnet of his car, she whisked everything back into her bag – and let him off with a caution. Now Joanna also happens to be a tall, statuesque beauty. Being a commercial traveller, the driver was forever ready to try his luck and he attempted to date her. She politely declined his offer but he nevertheless went away happily. Now no commercial traveller in the history of the internal combustion engine, has ever driven away from a brush with the male police 'happily'. Usually he is convinced that his name, address, description and company has been flashed to Interpol and is in the possession of every bloody copper from Land's End to John o'Groats.

When one considers the vulnerability of policewomen on the streets, it is surprising how few of them are actually injured in the course of their duty. On the other hand, it is amazing how many are injured in the station while carrying out such tasks as searching female prisoners. With both hands in the suspect's clothing and their bodies in close proximity, they can be extremely vulnerable. Many serious assaults have taken place on WPCs in this manner. In theory, there should be two officers present when someone is searched. This is as much for protection against any subsequent allegation against the searcher as for any great need for self-defence. But even with two officers present, it requires no great time to deliver a swift butt to the face, or knee to the groin.

Sometimes the assault will not even be physical. One young girl in her very first week of duty at Wharf Road was asked to search a well-built blonde who was believed to have drugs concealed in her underclothing. No matter what enquiries were made, the station officer was totally unable to obtain the services of another female to assist with the search. The young WPC therefore had no option but to begin the probe on her own. Two minutes later she emerged from the room looking quite ashen.

'Er, sergeant,' she faltered.

'Yeh,' grunted the station officer, reluctantly looking up from his mass of paper work.

'She's a he!'

I have been extremely fortunate never to have been present when an assault has taken place on a police girl. However, leaving the station very late one wild and stormy March night, I was on my way home along Walworth Road when I saw Bernadette, in what appeared to be great agony. She was staggering along the pavement, bent almost double, her hands clutched to her head. She appeared dazed and oblivious to the world around her. I instantly braked to a halt and ran over to her calling anxiously 'Bernie! Bernie! Are you all right?'

She appeared not to see me until I was almost touching her, then, looking up, her face broke into a lovely smile and she replied, 'Yeh! It's okay, Harry. It's just that the wind keeps blowing my bleedin' hat off!'

With all the problems and prejudices that the girls have faced and surmounted, I thought it would be interesting to speak with Beverley. Without any question, Bev is everybody's favourite. She has a magic disposition; one hardly ever sees her without a smile. She is competent, intelligent, shrewd *and* buxom. She is also very black.

I asked her if she had ever experienced any prejudices from her male colleagues in the few years that she had been in the force. She thought deeply for a while, then said:

'No, I can't say that I have.'

'Are you sure?' I persisted. 'No remarks about your physical appearance at all?'

'Well, perhaps in that case – yes.'

'What was it?' I said, reaching for my pen.

'They infer that I have big knockers,' she replied, with a smile about as wide as her bust-line.

The girls, then, like the poor, will always be with us; although they tend, as individuals, not to be with us for very long. A little over three years seems to be a fairly average stay. There is, therefore, a constantly changing scene. The reasons why they leave are as complex as the reasons why they join. They fall in love, which accounts for a few. They fall out of love, which accounts for a great deal more. They marry. They cannot abide night-duty, and lastly, unless they have moved into some of the more specialized departments, middle-aged ladies tend not to be keen on pounding the beat.

They have caused enormous changes in attitudes, from the youngest recruit to the highest ranks. There is constant controversy on the most efficient ratio of women to men that any one force should have. Arguments are endless but they are here to stay and I for one am quite happy about it. They not only look good but they make me laugh, and for me that is a real win-double.

''Ere, 'Arry mate, Hi 'eard this 'orrible scream, then Hi didn't 'ear nuffink else, Hi fink someone's 'ad an 'orrible haccident.'

Old May was in the habit of shuffling, countless times daily, up and down Chapel Street. I never did find out where she went to, but she always seemed determined to arrive there. A frail but tough old bird, with her long frock and threadbare carpet slippers she was as much a part of the local scene as the tenement buildings in which she lived. Her lifetime habit of never sounding the letter 'H', except always in the wrong place, had often caused me great amusement. Her carpet slippers formed another of her peculiarities. I knew May for over twenty years and during that period her slippers were always threadbare. I never knew her to possess a new pair, even at Christmas; she seemed to have access to an endless supply of worn carpet slippers.

May was a pleasant if slightly grimy lady, with a strange obsession with her hair. She was almost hag-like in the rest of her appearance, and her false teeth fitted badly. Yet her hair was always an immaculate platinum blonde, which, unfortunately, accentuated her 'slept-in' face.

'Where did this scream come from, May?' I asked.

'From the backs hof them 'ouses hover there, 'Arry mate.'

She pointed to a long row of terraced houses on the other side of the street. Each of these houses contained five families, one family per floor, plus one in the basement. May shuffled across the road with me to the position she was in when she first heard the scream. Feeling, no doubt, that she had done all that she could reasonably be expected to do, she then went about her daily business, whatever that was.

The houses in Chapel Street each shared communal front doors. There was often aggravation over this door. Some would always leave it open, others would always close it. If one occupier had left it open and popped keylessly around to the local shop, it would be safe to bet that on his return another inmate would have shut it. Noises, smells, kids, furniture-moving, stair-cleaning rotas, missing mail and prams in the passage, none of these bones of contention were in the same league as that bloody door.

My first call turned out to be the correct one. Number 37 Chapel Street had a fair cross-section of local types. On the third floor was a pleasant couple in their early fifties, of whom I knew very little except thar their divorced daughter lived on the second floor with her two sons. The first floor was occupied by Jeremiah Tomlinson, who, in spite of his name, was only in his late twenties. Jeremiah hated his name and seemed to hold the whole of society responsible for it; he was, therefore, one of our local villains. Jeremiah was also a failure. He had tried a whole range of crime and had yet to find a branch that he was any good at. He had spent half of his adult life in prison, but he had not only gained nothing – he'd also learnt nothing.

The ground floor was tenanted by the O'Connells, a quiet, hard-working couple whose three children attended the local Catholic Primary School. Finally, the basement was occupied by Sylvia, a single West Indian woman with two daughters aged nine and seven. Sylvia was employed in Guy's Hospital as a domestic help and often worked shifts. Unfortunately, both her girls suffered from a wanderlust and, given the opportunity, would frequently stroll away. 'Stroll' was exactly what they would do. They seemed to have no set plan, they would just wander down street after street until they were totally lost. They would never dream of turning back, they simply walked on until they were discovered, often twenty or so miles away.

Sylvia, as a result of this, developed the dangerous habit of locking both children indoors for the duration of all school holidays. All doors were locked from the outside and Sylvia kept the key. The children could not get out, nor could outsiders get in.

Both girls were at the window of the basement, anxiously waving to me and pointing to the rear of the house. There were french windows both to the back and front of the flat and, as possible compensation for living in the basement, the tenant was allowed the sole use of the rear garden. Unfortunately, access to this rear garden could only be gained via Sylvia's locked doors. These opened on to a concreted area with a flight of stone steps leading up to garden level.

I entered 37 through the open communal door and, after half-heartedly trying Sylvia's door, began to ascend the interior staircase. When I reached the rear windows of the first floor, I found one ajar and deep scuff marks in the paintwork. I casually put my head out of the window and, in the basement area some twenty feet below, saw what looked like a crumpled body.

I clattered down the stairs and tried Sylvia's door with a renewed energy. I called to the two children: 'Open the door, kids.'

'We can't, Mum's got the key,' came back the predictable reply.

I ran quickly to number 39 and knocked frantically on the basement door. It was opened eventually by a plump young mum, breastfeeding her offspring. I gave a garbled explanation and ran through the flat into the rear garden.

Each garden was separated by a three-foot wall topped with a further three feet of wooden fencing. I quickly scaled this fence and dropped down into the garden of number 37, almost falling down the area staircase. The crumpled unconscious figure, I discovered, was none other than Jeremiah Tomlinson. Jeremiah was in a very bad way. He lay face down on the concrete floor and his back was badly twisted between a rusty old lawn mower and the area staircase. I could neither hear breathing nor find a heartbeat. Blood trickled from his mouth, he reeked of scotch and looked much too injured for me to move.

I used my personal radio to call for an ambulance and requested the still bare-breasted mum from next door to watch for it. Meanwhile, I returned to keep guard over the rapidly expiring Jeremiah. I became aware that he had something clutched in his right hand. I pressed it open and discovered an old round-ended kitchen knife. What the hell would Jeremiah be lying here for with an old kitchen knife? Of course! My quick search of his clothing confirmed what I had suspected – no keys! Jeremiah had returned home after a drinking bout, without his keys. Being a professional burglar – albeit not a very good one – he decided to climb into his own bedroom window, but then he had fallen! What sort of a burglar is it that can't break into his own flat?

A call from the next garden indicated that the ambulance crew had arrived. They negotiated the fence, not without some difficulty, and eventually laid the stretcher alongside the now apparently dead Jeremiah.

'There's not much point in being too careful with this one,' said the senior of the two ambulance men. 'If we don't get him into casualty soon, he's a goner – providing he's not dead already!'

They began to roll Jeremiah rather unceremoniously on to the vacant stretcher. I always feel helpless in the presence of ambulance crews. Their competence gives me a terrible inferiority complex. Then I tend to do silly things. I now did a beaut!

I decided that their task would be made a great deal easier if the old lawn mower was moved. I balanced on the wall above the stretcher and lifted the mower by its long handle. Unfortunately, I was not standing immediately above the mower but about two feet to its left. It weighed a great deal more than I anticipated and as soon as it cleared the ground, it began an unstoppable pendulum-like swing. The soft 'clunk' as it struck Jeremiah's head caused me to relinquish my hold instantly. It fell on the foot of the older of the two stretcher-bearers.

'Have you ever been a brain-surgeon?' said the man acidly, as he curled his foot up in agony.

'Oh well, I should think you've just done him,' said his young companion cheerfully. He bent closely over the motionless figure of Jeremiah. 'Still, he don't look no worse – and he don't look no better. He's got so many problems that a simple skull fracture will almost go unnoticed,' he added matter-of-factly.

'I – I'm – terribly sorry,' I stammered. 'It was a bit heavier than . . .'

'That's all right, mate, happens all the time with your blokes. Like bulls in china shops some of 'em are.'

It struck me that the younger one was an extremely forgiving bloke, but then he had emerged unscathed. His senior partner did not look very happy, and as for Jeremiah – well, he just looked very dead.

'Just give us a hand to clear this fence,' said the old one, bristly.

Three stout leather straps held the patient firmly on the stretcher as we swung it into the garden of number 39. I helpfully held open the door that led into the basement flat and paused to thank the lady occupier for her co-operation. She was sitting in an armchair with junior suckling, this time at the other breast.

'This is a right bleedin' mad street, this one,' said the still limping ambulance driver. 'Burglars who can't break into their own bloody flats; coppers who throw sodding lawn mowers at you; and topless mums!'

I accompanied the ambulance to the hospital where, because there was a surprising spark of life, the apparently deceased was rushed into the intensive care unit; here he was to remain for some eight days. His catalogue of injuries was interesting. It read like a medical student's nightmare. There were, of course, numerous contusions and abrasions. In addition the fractures consisted of ribs, knee-caps, forearm, jaw, pelvis and skull! Within nine months Jeremiah Tomlinson was not only healed but had been arrested for breaking and entering!

The core of Jeremiah's trouble was that he simply never learnt anything. Once he felt completely fit again he decided to join his old associate John-John McGuire in a little jewellery theft. Now if Jeremiah was not over-bright, he was a mathematical physicist in comparison to John-John. When I once asked him why McGuire was called John-John, he said, in all apparent seriousness, that he (McGuire) was so thick that he never understood the first John!

After sinking a few pints in the Duke of Sutherland, both villains had scaled the wall surrounding the rear yard of the Wharf Road branch of the Royal Arsenal Co-operative Society.

'We'll just shift a bit of jewellery,' John-John had said.

Considering the state of the pair of them, they gained access remarkably well, but of course as soon as they entered the building the alarm was set off.

'Can you hear a bell?' Jeremiah had said.

'No,' answered John-John.

'Well, I can. Go outside and listen.'

John-John then dutifully left the premises and stood in

the yard listening to the bell that was now ringing loud and clear in the late evening air. Somehow he convinced himself that the bell he could hear was not the Co-op's at all, but belonged to Woolworth's on the opposite side of the road. He then climbed back in the store!

'Honestly, Harry,' Jeremiah told me the next day, 'we were legless. Co-op jewellery! It's worth about ninepence a ton!'

The following morning saw him treading a well-worn path to Camberwell Green Magistrates' Court where a rather charitable magistrate fined him £25.

'I was well pleased, Harry, I can tell yer. He's a nutter, that John-John, I'll never do a screw-in with him again!'

It was at this stage that Jeremiah's luck, such as it was, ran out. While he was being dealt with at the Magistrates' Court, a rather sharp-eyed detective sergeant recognized him from an outstanding burglary two years earlier. The detective returned to his station and looked up the relevant Crime Book entry and three days later Jeremiah was being remanded to Crown Court on three charges of burglary and one of assault.

'On my life, sergeant, I didn't do it,' pleaded Jeremiah with all of the sincerity that he could muster at so short a notice. Now, 'On my life, sergeant, I didn't do it,' is, in villain's jargon, a straightforward confession of guilt. It translates into police jargon roughly as, 'It's a fair cop, guv'nor,' or, 'Okay, I know you have your job to do.' There are several different levels of verbal confessions. They vary only in the intensity with which the villain in question wishes to avoid his come-uppance. Slightly higher up the scale is probably, 'On my mother's grave'. This means that although he actually committed the crime and *he* knows that *you* know that he did it, he is not going to admit anything, at least until he knows just how strong your evidence is. As a general rule, the users of this phrase either (a) never knew their mother, (b) didn't wish to know her, (c) stole from her purse regularly, (d) mugged her, or (e) occasionally got on quite well with her.

The final protestation is the absolute hundred-per-cent acknowledgement of guilt. But because he has at least one suspended sentence hanging over him, he is not going to play ball with you. He then comes out with the number one gilt-edged confession in any policeman's book: 'On my baby's life I didn't do it.' If this oath has any credence at all, then heaven must be littered with little cockney tots, all just waiting for their dads who sent them there some seventy years too early.

Yes, 'On my life . . .' was serious but not quite terminal.

The sergeant was not without his own problems, however. With any charge so ancient in time, one has the witnesses to consider. There was plenty of evidence to convict Jeremiah: after all he had never been a subtle thief and traces of him were absolutely everywhere at the scene of the crime. But the witness had been so sure of Jeremiah's identity that most of the case for the prosecution revolved around this identification. This 'cast-iron' witness, however –not for the first time –'went bent'. You can be sure that just as soon as the chief prosecution witness prefaces his replies with sentences like 'I'm not *really* sure but . . .', 'Well, it *could* have been him . . .', 'I *thought* it looked like him . . .' and 'Well it *was* dark . . .' everyone in the court begins to gather up their papers for an early finish.

'Not guilty,' said the foreman of the jury.

'When you have recovered from your surprise you may leave the dock,' said the judge.

'That comes of spoiling a good case with an eye-witness,' said the detective sergeant.

Jeremiah was once again a free man.

'A party! That's what we'll have!' exclaimed John-John,

as Jeremiah and several of his friends gathered in the large entrance-hall of the Crown Court.

The rest of the tenants in 37 Chapel Street groaned in anticipation as they saw the two taxis stop outside the front door. They had experienced Jeremiah's coming-out parties before. By 9.30 p.m. the party was in full-swing. By 11.30 p.m. Jeremiah was quite dead, having choked first on a chicken-bone and secondly on his own vomit.

Now if there is one thing that the underworld enjoys more than a good coming-out party, it's a good funeral. These occasions are always superbly planned and no expense is spared, no matter who is going to pay for it. Jeremiah Tomlinson's funeral was no exception. The only surprise to me was the choice of undertakers. Sid Crouch, the local Wharf Road mortician, was highly regarded among the underworld fraternity. ('Always does a good show, does Sid.') But, as John-John said to me a few days later, 'I fort it would be a real nice touch to 'ave the Co-op, Mr Cole. Jeremiah would've liked that – sort of poetic, you'd call it. Besides, they promised to do a lovely turn-out.'

Ten Co-op funeral cars and a hundred and fifty wreaths set back the economy of the criminal fraternity quite a bit, but it was well worth it. It was indeed a 'lovely turn-out'.

I decided to escort the leading cars along the Walworth Road in order to facilitate the traffic. After all, the hearse moved very slowly and I had no trouble keeping ahead of it on my cycle. The route to Streatham cemetery was direct: turn south into Walworth Road and keep going for about five miles. I had intended to accompany the cortège as far as Camberwell Green, about one mile in distance and near the border of our manor. Just before the leading car reached the Green, it surprisingly turned left.

'Where are you going, mate?' I called across to the driver.

'Peckham,' he answered.

'Peckham?' I echoed. 'But that's a couple of miles' detour.'

'I know, but they want us to stop for a minute's silence outside his favourite bingo hall.'

How touching, I felt. Or it would have been had Jeremiah ever been a bingo player; but he wasn't. He was just a 'dip' (pickpocket) who worked the queues at the bus-stop outside the hall and the gaming machines inside.

I stopped by the side of the road and sat thoughtfully on my cycle as the last of the cars purred by towards Peckham. It's not very much to show for a life. Twenty-nine years of age, eight of which had been spent in prison, and a minute's silence outside a bingo hall. I looked at my watch. It was a little after 1 p.m. I suddenly realized how hungry I was. I turned my cycle around and began to return to Wharf Road Police Station for lunch. I could have taken any of several routes back but I decided to return via Chapel Street. As I passed number 37 it looked strangely different. At first glance I couldn't fathom why. Then I suddenly realized. For the first time in my experience, the front door was closed. There's no doubt about it, Jeremiah, they don't want you back.

'Castlewine' was one of urban society's greatest mistakes – a high-rise block. It is about as long as it is tall and massively ugly. If it were stood on its side (and that was often suggested) no one would know the difference. It was also the first building in the area to drop the name 'House'. It was part of the social thinking at the time of its conception: Castlewine sounds far more exclusive, even more glamorous than Castlewine House.

The interiors of the flats were, in fact, excellent, but the design of the overall structure was just short of disastrous. Apart from being some twenty storeys high, the corridors on each floor were long and windowless. They were a nightmare for families with young children. To let a toddler play downstairs in the yard, often out of sight and out of hearing, was too much for most young mothers. The children could therefore play in the corridors and on the interior emergency staircase. This, in turn, created the further problem of noise and nuisance. To childless tenants and those whose children had long been forgotten, they were just one more problem to be endured and suffered.

One hundred and fifty feet up from ground level, three-year-old Mandy Rodgers arranged her dolls in two neat lines across a couple of Castlewine steps. Mandy lived on the twelfth floor and was an only child. Her friend Debbie, who lived just three doors along, was unfortunately confined to her flat with ominous-looking spots. Mandy was hoping for a similar outbreak herself. An overnight rash would give her at least a reasonable chance of playing with Debbie's doll's pram. Being the dominating partner of the relationship, Mandy found it easy to convince Debbie that a long play with a paper cut-out theatre (total cost about £1) was infinitely more desirable than any exclusive use of a shiny new red and silver doll's pram (value about twenty-five quid). Mandy, being a shrewd little miss, was well aware she was getting the best of the bargain. Debbie, on the other hand, had a feeling she was being had over, but, on balance, considered Mandy's friendship just about worth it.

Mrs Jean Rodgers, a slight, pretty young woman, was preparing Sunday lunch. Her husband Tony was at the pub and fairly certain to remain there until it closed at two o'clock. With her wall-to-wall Valium, Jean was becoming increasingly neurotic about her flat in the sky. Every few minutes she would trot to her front door and call anxiously to Mandy:

'Are you all right, love?'

Mandy, who considered this whole drill to be quite tiresome, would dutifully reply:

'Y-E-S, mum.'

Mrs Rodgers was not at all happy about the child being on the staircase. She was, after all, out of sight. But a kid couldn't spend the whole day in the flat. It would be worse than a prison.

Jean had just rinsed a milk bottle and, although it wasn't yet time for one of her front-door excursions, thought it would be less effort to place the bottle outside than attempt to find room for it on the already overcrowded draining board. As she stooped and placed the bottle on the corridor floor, she was tempted to call yet again to Mandy. On the other hand, Mandy did not like the calls to be too frequent.

'Big girls' mummies aren't always calling out to them,' the child would say, reproachfully.

She was about to push the door to, when a piercing scream cut through to her stomach, as swift and as sharp as any razor. It was not a scream of play, it was a scream of unmitigated terror – and it was Mandy's scream.

Jean tried hard to run but her legs refused to move. 'Oh no! Oh no!' she could hear herself saying. After what seemed an eternity, she reached the steps. All she could see was an assortment of disarranged dolls. Their wide blank stares seemed to be part of the overall terror.

'Mandy! Mandy! Mandy!' screamed Jean.

'Momma, momma, momma,' echoed the talking doll that had plunged forward, thereby triggering off its own mechanism.

Leaping over the dolls, tripping and staggering up the first stair-flight, she rounded the corner to find another empty set of stairs. Breathlessly she climbed them. Again, nothing.

'Oh God! I've gone the wrong way!'

Down again, slipping, sliding, she scattered the dolls for the second time.

'Momma, momma, momma,' croaked the doll.

'M-A-N-D-Y!!' screamed Jean.

Just one flight down and around the corner she found a bundle, or rather a whimpering little blood-stained heap.

'Mike 3! Mike 3! Twelfth floor Castlewine. Serious indecent assault on a child. Suspect believed close by. No flat number given. Informant too distressed. Message ends, 1315!'

'That's the fourth assault on a kid in that block this year!' I exclaimed to my two crew members, 'Bootsie' Hill the radio operator and Derek Blake the observer. I was, of course, at the extreme end of the manor and I would have to negotiate three miles of Sunday lunchtime drivers in order to arrive at the scene.

'In all my years on this bloody car, I've never had a

serious call without I haven't been at the opposite end of the ground,' I complained as I snaked my way through the double roundabout at the Elephant and Castle.

'You always say that,' answered Bootsie. 'Why don't you try beginning the day by driving in the opposite direction?'

The gear-box of the Wolseley 110 screeched in protest as I chicaned my way through the parked cars and derelict vehicles that littered the yard of Castlewine. Braking to a halt, all three of us slammed our doors in unison as we ran for the two lifts. One was out of action and the other was being used by the milkman – bloody marvellous! We rushed for the staircase and, leaping three steps at a time, rapidly scaled the first few flights. There was, however, a definite slowing at the third floor and by the time we reached the tenth the blood was pounding in my head. Gasping for breath, we staggered along the twelfth-floor corridor and, seeing the first open door, ran in. The penetrating sobs told us we had guessed correctly.

The first door on the right was the bathroom. Kneeling beside the bath was the source of the sobs. Mrs Rodgers was bathing her daughter, in some symbolic attempt to wash away the memory of the last few minutes. Every few seconds, the white-faced child would push out her arms, hold herself rigid and emit an awful dry, hoarse scream.

'It's all right, love, it's all right. Mummy's here. No one is going to hurt you now,' soothed the woman, between sobs.

Hearing us enter, she turned, and in the time that it took her to make that simple movement, she changed. She changed from a calm, mollifying, gentle creature into a baggage of hate. Hatred, the like of which I had never seen before. A hatred which, although I well understood, and in fact almost shared, frightened me in its intensity.

'The bastard! The bastard!' she hissed. 'I'll kill him! I'll cut him into shreds and make him eat them! I'll push him from the top of this building! Look! He's stained my baby! Oh I'll have him! I'll have him all right, even if I have to wait twenty years! No court's going to let him get away with this. I'll kill the bastard, I tell you! – I'll kill him ! ! !'

With that, she threw herself across the bath and embraced the child as if she wished her to return to the sanctuary of the very womb from whence she came.

We three looked at each other in helpless frustration. Knowing how she felt, we also knew that in a case of rape or indecent assault, she was doing the worst possible, albeit most understandable, thing: she was bathing the child!

We knew, of course, that if we had been in her position, we would have been doing exactly the same. Yet swabs had to be taken. Just how *can* one clinically preserve any molested child until that can be accomplished? The evidence was disappearing fast and none of us had the courage to stop it.

'Her knickers! Where are they?' exclaimed Derek.

'I don't know, they must still be on the staircase. I'll burn them,' cried Jean angrily.

Derek ran out of the flat, and Bootsie and I began to coax her to remove Mandy from the bath.

'Come on, luv,' I pleaded. 'She must go to hospital. She needs to be examined.'

'She's dirty, he's stained her. He's stained my baby,' she kept repeating.

Her voice was losing much of its venom. She now spoke quietly, between sobs.

'Why? Tell me why. Why to my baby? Look at her. She's just a mite, a toddler. Who'd want to hurt her?' Her voice began to rise again. 'Who'd want to hurt my baby?'

With the last few pleading words she plucked the child from the water and wrapped her swiftly in a large white towel. Clutching the bundle tightly to her, she despairingly buried her smooth face into my rough tunic and cried an absolute flood of tears.

Derek soon returned, in company with two ambulance men. He had removed his cap and was now holding it in his hand. Partially concealed inside it was a white pair of blood- and semen-stained child's knickers.

Mrs Rodgers would not let Mandy be placed on a stretcher. For that matter, neither would Mandy agree to be placed. Therefore, with a red blanket around her shoulders, Jean cradled her child down to the ambulance, via the now mercifully vacant lift.

There was one question we had to ask Mandy – we had postponed it long enough.

'Mandy, luv, did you know the naughty man that hurt you?'

The child did not react at all. She stared at me for a moment, then buried her face as deeply as she could into her mother's neck.

King's College Hospital casualty department was its usual chaotic self. A typical inner-city hospital, it never seemed short of the walking wounded. There were the endless talking drunks with the deep abrasions and filthy clothes. The Sunday park footballers sat forlornly on a bench, still clad in their shorts and jerseys, with only the bootless foot to denote which ankle was broken. There was the do-it-yourselfer whose ladder had slipped. Little four-year-old Dean, whose exploring fingers had explored yet another closing gap, cried quietly in the corner. There were the sick; the lame; the confused; the complaining; the patient; the sleeping; the forgotten. And now there was Mandy.

A brief explanation to the Sister-in-charge, and both mother and child were swiftly ushered into a small ante-room. Within a couple of minutes, a young female doctor, who looked just a little over fifteen years old, followed them into the room. She wore a white coat that could have been made for a very large brother. We had left Derek at the scene in a vain search for witnesses, and since there was now little that Bootsie and I could accomplish at the hospital, we decided to rejoin him.

The lift door scraped open and we stepped out on to the twelfth-floor corridor. Bootsie walked towards the Rodgers' flat, but I decided to have a look around the staircase. There was really nothing to be seen but at least I'd feel better having checked. After a fruitless search, I decided to pick up the dolls from the staircase. I scooped them into my arms. 'Momma, momma, momma,' chimed the talking doll. Returning to the flat, I deposited them all on to Mandy's bed.

'Whadda you want?' said a sharp voice.

I turned to see the bleary features of a young man who had quietly followed me into the flat. He was barely in his twenties. While he wasn't actually drunk, he was about as close as it is possible to get.

'Who are you, guv?' I queried.

'I live here.'

'I'm sure you do, but what's your name?' I insisted.

'Rodgers. Why?'

'Do you have a daughter, Mandy?'

'Yes. Why? What's happened?'

'I'm sorry, but she's had an accident. Well, no, actually – well, she's not had an accident, she's been assaulted – indecently assaulted,' I blurted apologetically.

'Where is she now?' he demanded.

'King's College Hospital. Come on, I'll run you up there,' I offered.

'If you bastards had done your job properly this wouldn't have happened,' he hissed. 'If you had stopped persecuting motorists like me, I could have driven up there myself. But no, I'm disqualified! I'm disqualified after just a couple of drinks. If you stopped persecuting us motorists, you might start to catch a few of these fucking murderers and then our kids might be safe on the streets. You blokes make me fucking sick,' he said vehemently.

The warning bells that every policemen has locked away in his head were beginning to sound. The situation had definitely reached a dangerous stage. Many drunks will respond to reason; three-quarter-drunks never do. I knew I shouldn't lose my temper. I also knew I was about to.

'Listen, you obnoxious little prick. I don't catch murderers because they are much too clever for me. I can only catch bloody idiots like you. Now, do you want a lift to King's Hospital or don't you? Your child is badly hurt and your wife is half out of her mind! Are you staying here, or are you going there? It's as simple as that. But if you talk to me again like . . .'

Bootsie and Derek hastened into the room at the sound of our raised voices. It was obvious that Mr Rodgers had had no idea they were there.

'Oh, that's your game, is it? Go on, kick me! Beat me up! I don't care what you do, I'm not going to that hospital with you. I'll crawl on my hands and knees first!' he snarled.

'What's the matter with this bloke, is he a nutter?' asked Bootsie.

'He's half pissed and hateful,' I answered. 'There isn't much more we can do here anyway, so we'll leave him to it. I would have thought, though, he'd want to be with his kid at a time like this.'

'I'm-not-pissed!' yelled the father, his voice rising with every syllable. With that, he made a lunge towards me, but was immediately seized by Derek, who simply threw him back on to Mandy's bed. He made no further move but just lay on the bed, breathing deeply and glaring at me.

'You've made a friend there,' said Bootsie as we walked towards the lift.

A couple of minutes later we were down in the yard. I groaned to see that an old green Ford Consul had completely boxed in the police car. There was no sign of the driver. I tried all four doors of the vehicle but they were securely locked.

No policeman (or crook) spent more than a couple of minutes gaining access to an old Ford and soon Derek was releasing the handbrake. Slowly we rolled back the car and I heard Derek re-apply the brake. He emerged from the driver's seat studying a brown envelope. Without a word, he handed it to me. It was a tax demand, addressed to a Mr Anthony Rodgers. The same Anthony Rodgers, no doubt, who had followed us into his flat. The same Anthony Rodgers who had boxed us in with his car. But didn't he say he was disqualified?

We heard the lift door slide open again. Tony Rodgers was very surprised to see us still on the premises.

'You boxed us in with *your* car,' I said pointedly.

'It's not my car!' he predictably countered.

'Well, I'd have a word with the owner, then, 'cos he's nicking your mail,' said Derek quietly.

'I'm sorry, fellas,' he said, offering his hand. 'I had a couple of drinks and I always fly off the handle when I get upset. Will you still take me to King's?'

I was about to revel in the last word, when I decided against it, and soon we were back in the maelstrom of King's casualty department. I was just in time to catch a glimpse of the young doctor as she studiously pressed a footballer's puffy ankle.

'Doctor!' I called.

She looked up.

'How's the little girl?'

She looked me straight in the eyes and said curtly and without emotion:

'There was considerable penetration.'

Oh God, no! I felt suddenly ashamed. Ashamed to be a

member of the same sex and civilization as the perpetrator of this outrage.

We three returned to the station in complete silence. This was very unusual; we were normally a chatty crew, but both Derek and I had daughters of approximately Mandy's age. I thought of how I would feel if it had been my child. Jean Rodgers was right. I would have wanted to kill him, whoever 'him' was. Bootsie was the first one to break the silence.

'You know, he's simply got to live in Castlewine.'

'Why?' I asked.

'Well, surely no one could, or would, go up to the twelfth floor, at one o'clock on a Sunday afternoon, attack a child and vanish? Not unless they lived there!'

'Let's look up the other attacks,' I suggested.

That proved to be no easy matter. In fact, we were unable to complete the search for several days. My original observation had been that this was the fourth attack that year. But the search revealed that this was only the third in three years. Nevertheless, each attack had been on a child on or near the staircase. Also, after each attack the culprit had escaped by going either up or down the stairs.

Castlewine received quite a hammering from police for a few days. House-to-house enquiries were made; almost everyone living in the block was interviewed; records were checked; snap searches of lifts, staircases and corridors were carried out. Result: nothing. In fact, there were no further assaults, or leads, for another four years.

I had by this time ceased being an area car driver and had become a community copper. I arrived for late-turn duty one day to be told that there was a twenty-year-old youth in the charge room. He had been caught exposing himself to young children in nearby Kennington Park. I looked in the room, mainly out of curiosity and also to check if I knew him. I didn't.

'Where's he live?' I asked the young detective constable who had arrested him.

He glanced down at his papers. 'Castlewine,' he said.

I looked at the prisoner with renewed interest. I couldn't help but feel what a sad little lad he was. He looked at us with wide, almost worshipful eyes and seemed eager to please. Unlike so many prisoners who are arrested for sexual offences he did not appear in any way nervous. He sat very upright on the bare wooden bench, his hands clasped neatly together in his lap. Whatever school or institution he had attended, he had obviously been regularly instructed to 'sit up straight'. This he now did. He reminded me of a dutiful little dog. His simple face perfectly reflected his simple mind.

'We had three very bad assaults on kids in Castlewine a year or two back,' I said to his captor.

'I did that,' smiled the simpleton.

'You did what ?' said the detective.

'I did what that man said I did. I didn't hurt them though. I just played with their thingies. And then they bleeded, so I got frightened and run.'

A few quick enquiries revealed what had happened, and why he was never discovered in our search four years earlier.

Peter Davidson had been on home leave to his parents, who lived on the fourteenth floor of Castlewine. They were possibly slightly less simple than Peter, and when the house-to-house enquiries were made they answered truthfully, but misleadingly: 'Yes', they were the only two occupants of the flat; 'No', no one else lived there. On the Tuesday of the enquiry, that was in fact true, Peter was not there – he had returned to his hostel the day before.

I remember wishing Peter had been caught without my knowledge. On the day that Mandy was raped, I had wanted to kill him. All my emotions and feelings had been aimed at him – whoever 'him' was. Now I'd met him and I just felt so sorry for him. Why wasn't he a beast, or a drooling evil monster? Why couldn't he be a sly, despicable, gloating coward? Why did he have to be a wide-eyed smiling simpleton?

All of society, including the police force, placates itself with child molesters. We can safely hate the perpetrators. 'I don't mind a good crook, providing they don't hurt anyone. It's the child molesters that I can't stand.' Oh, it's so easy. Never mind about the rest of the victims. If we use all our hatred on the attackers of children we can all feel quite noble. Sometimes I just feel that is cheating. Sometimes a single crime has many victims and no perpetrator.

Seven-year-old Mandy Rodgers seems happily to have forgotten that Sunday. Jean Rodgers never will. The drunken appearance of her husband was the final nail in their coffin of a marriage. With the marriage in tatters and her child raped, Jean had a breakdown. She has now fully recovered but she still considers, rightly or wrongly, that her reluctance to call to Mandy when she placed down the bottle changed her whole life.

Anthony Rodgers is now an alcoholic. He can often be seen on the benches in Camberwell Green. Who's to say he was ever destined to be anything else?

Peter Davidson's life would have been made hell in a prison, but he fortunately didn't go there. Instead, he was remanded back to an institution where he now sits up straight and smiles his simple smile.

House of Ill Repute

The church clock of St Mark's began to strike 3 a.m. The first chime quavered overlong on the still night air. The second paused impatiently, waiting for all traces of its predecessor to fade. Then it, too, pompously announced its own arrival to a sleeping and indifferent borough. As the third stroke trembled its way over the smoky roof-tops, I wondered just how I would survive the next three hours. I was absolutely exhausted. That afternoon I had played in a football cup-tie which had run into extra time. My legs felt like lead.

I watched in fascination for a while, as a group of cats played out some eerie feline ritual in the centre of the deserted street. This was their time of day. Sitting in a quiet circle, they stared at each other, oblivious to any other species, be it a passing policeman or a mumbling drunk.

There in the back streets, the silence of that hour is absolute. The last of the late-night revellers are slipping between their chill, damp sheets, and the early morning cleaners have yet to reach for their brass-belled alarm clocks. It is almost as if time itself is taking a breather. Yesterday is dead and tomorrow not yet born.

I was posted that night to 7 Beat, probably the least desired of all our fifteen beats. It was triangular in shape. A rather bleak stretch of the Old Kent Road formed the left side of the triangle. This was joined at a bridge by the long, derelict Grand Surrey Canal which formed the right side. The base line was Cockburn Road, which ran straight from the Old Kent Road, to peter out disappointingly, back at the canal.

The interior of the beat was equally uninspiring: a tiny park, a bus garage, a long line of dead factories whose arteries had been cut when the canal was closed, and an assortment of small, tree-lined streets. 7 Beat was excruciatingly boring, but it was also the best-kept area on the whole of our manor. The houses were mainly Victorian or Edwardian, without as much as a single block of flats to be seen. I found myself walking down Cockburn Road and instinctively heading towards the bus garage. The canteen at the garage opened around 3.30 a.m. and the enamel-removing tea would at least be hot. I would have sold my soul for a cup of tea.

Each front garden that I passed was well kept, with neatly trimmed hedges and well painted gates. Yet the one thing that always impressed me about Cockburn Road was the dustbins – you couldn't see them. To me, dustbins are the usual sign of urban decay and in Cockburn Road they were all carefully hidden! The occupiers of this road were little different from the residents of any of the other hundred or so streets and alleys that we policed. They followed the same kinds of occupation and very few of the houses were privately owned. It was just that they were geographically fortunate and this gave the street its status.

The only stain on the street's good name was the mystery of number 110a. The front door of this two-up and two-down house was almost adjacent to the school wall, and was recessed, making it difficult to see any 'comings or goings'. A scandal had burst in the street some three months before, when the occupier, the jovial Mr Johnny Lewis, had been bundled unceremoniously into a police van. Amazingly enough, no one in the street knew why, that was, until the local paper found out, then they all knew why. 'Jolly' Johnny Lewis had been keeping a brothel! A brothel in Cockburn Road! Well, I ask you! Talk about letting the tone of the street down. No wonder he was always so bloody jolly!

Since that date, the house had been locked up. Mr Lewis had written from prison to our Superintendent asking for police to pay some attention to his property. As he so rightly stated in his brief letter, 'You can't trust anyone these days.' Jolly Johnny was, allowing for good behaviour, about half-way through his nine-month sentence, so 110a Cockburn Road was, in the main, yesterday's news.

For the second time that night, I glanced at the bay windows of 110a. The front door had so many huge padlocks attached that there was little danger of entry at that point. The windows, however, were much more vulnerable. As I looked my heartbeat quickened. On my previous check of the premises, around midnight, I had placed an empty milk bottle on the window sill. It was no longer there! A cat perhaps? God knows there were enough of them about. I quietly looked around the overgrown front garden. There it was, next to the tall, wavering mass of Michaelmas daisies. It wasn't broken, nor lying on its side, it was standing neatly to attention. Now there were some pretty weird cats in that road, but not one of them, I was prepared to bet, would go around standing up milk bottles.

What to do? I quickly worked out a 'for and against' list.

For going in

1. The intruders may have spotted me and if I delayed they may therefore escape. (It was before the days of personal radio, so there was little chance of any immediate help.)
2. To give evidence in court about a person found actually present in the house sounded infinitely

better than someone you may have seen legging it across the garden.

Against going in

1. I had no idea how many were in there.
2. It was dark.
3. I had no torch.
4. I was on my own.
5. Most important of all, I may receive a thumping.

The 'against' won by an overwhelming majority.

The clip-clop of high heels on a pavement interrupted my parliamentary deliberations and I saw stepping briskly down Cockburn Road a young early morning cleaner. I knew she would be making her way to the all-night bus-stop in Old Kent Road. Almost opposite the police box!

I called quietly to her. Up until that moment she was obviously unaware of my presence – and my voice gave her a hell of a fright.

'Bleedin' 'ell, mate! You scared the bleedin' daylights outa me!'

'Shssssss,' I whispered. I explained that I wanted her to lift up the receiver in the police box and ask whoever answered for some assistance at this address.

''Ere,' she said curtly, 'I 'ope I don't miss my bleedin' bus frew you! My fore-lady will do her nut if I do. I was twice late last week.'

'If she asks you, just say that you was helping some bloke to climb into a brothel. That should shut her up,' I answered.

'Is that what y'are trying to do? Why, you randy sod! You'll probably find my old man in there,' she added, as she hastened cheerfully away.

The time dragged as I waited for the assistance to arrive and soon St Mark's was chiming out yet another hour.

After a few more minutes, I heard a faint metallic creaking noise which became increasingly close.

'Oh, no!' I said, almost out loud. 'Not him, please!' I knew exactly who, or rather what, the noise was. It was Jock Tiffleck on his rusty old bike. That cycle had a unique creak; I think he used wet grit as a lubricant. Jock was a big, burly, red-faced Scot. He was the most impartial man I have ever met in my life – he hated everybody. He had joined the force around 1935 and everyone who had ever worked with him had been wishing him out ever since. Jock Tiffleck was a throw-back to Robert the Bruce and Bannockburn. He really belonged at the top of a glen, swishing his claymore and slaughtering the English. He had the charm and grace of Attila the Hun and the finesse of a three-legged rhino. Someone at Wharf Road had shown a great sense of humour: I required a David and they sent me Goliath.

Propping his cycle against the wall, he turned his attention to me.

'Wassamatter wi' ye, laddie? I hope ye hav'na git me heere on a fool's errand,' he boomed.

I looked at him and sighed. He possessed the longest police raincoat that I ever saw. He stood well over six feet and the coat almost reached his ankles. All that could be seen beneath its hem were his huge boots and a tantalizing glimpse of cycle clip. I couldn't think of anyone less suited to slip quietly into a brothel.

I gave Jock a quick run-down on what had happened. Now, in fairness to him, the one aspect in which he really excelled was in sniffing out crooks. He was genuinely impossible to con. His formula for this was absolutely foolproof, he just didn't believe anything anyone ever told him. Once he had examined the window, he did not require me to tell him something was wrong. *I* had needed that disturbed milk bottle: it was tangible, first it was here, then it was there. Jock scorned any such games. He worked entirely on instinct, and it rarely let him down.

'Someone's in heere, laddie, und theer's many o' theem,' he growled.

'Shall I go down to the police box and . . .?'

'Nae! Theer's two o' us isn't theer? Come on alonga me. Wee'll soon sort this bunch ooout!'

He spread his great palms flat on the window pane and pushed upwards. Slowly the window began to move.

I slipped quietly and easily over the sill. Jock clambered over it. His helmet, which he rarely removed from his head, dislodged both the curtains and the heavy rod that they were attached to. As they crashed down on to his shoulders, he uttered some obscure Gaelic oath.

'There surely can't be anyone still here after the noise we've made,' I said ruefully.

'Thee're ste-e-el heere a'right,' he grunted as he led me into the back of the house.

Jock's official police torch was as useless as mine. Also like mine, it was back at the station, so we followed the weak yellow light of his cycle lamp. We had soon covered the whole of the ground level and there was only the next floor to check. We climbed the twelve carpeted stairs and each tried the door handles of the two bedrooms. Jock's was locked; mine opened about an inch but would go no further. There was obviously something propped behind the door. I pulled the door shut and then threw it sharply open – almost in one movement. There was a hell of a crash and I fell over the chair that had been propped against the door handle.

Jock took a couple of quick strides and joined me in the room. As I climbed to my knees, I followed with my eyes the faint light of his lamp. On the back of the chair that had been propped against the door was a uniform jacket with the words 'United States Air Force' boldly emblazoned on the shoulder. The room, or what little of it could be seen in that pathetic glare, appeared none too clean. A noise from behind the door caused Jock to swing his torch swiftly around.

At right angles to the open door and close to the wall was a rumpled bed. In the bed lay a woman of about thirty. On top of her, totally oblivious to any interruptions, was a huge black man!

'Evening, lovelies. What can I do for you?' she cooed, in a lilting Welsh accent.

'You can get yon laddie off you for a start,' said Jock.

She removed a bare arm from the bedclothes and tapped the black man on the shoulder.

'Hey, Choc'y! Get off for a minute, there's a lovely.'

Choc'y did.

'Who are you and what are you doing here?' I asked. Which in view of the circumstances sounded peculiarly naïve.

'I'm Gladys and we're engaged, lovely. Aren't we, Choc'y, aren't we engaged?'

Choc'y did not seem at all sure.

'Who's in the other room?'

'My sister Freda with her bloke.'

'What's his name?'

'Joe.'

'Are they engaged?'

'Of course, lovely.'

'I thought they might be.'

Jock went back to the other bedroom and pounded heavily on the door. There was no reply. Choc'y struck a match and, reaching out, lit a candle that was standing on a white chipped saucer, on a dressing table beneath the window.

Suddenly Gladys threw back the clothes and, totally naked, joined Jock at the locked bedroom door.

'Come on, Freda. Open the door, lovely. I'm bloody freezing!'

I had thought the Negro had been big, but Gladys was

truly massive. She had an assortment of tattoos scattered over her body. I could not see them all, but four large butterflies winged their way around her navel, a large snake disappeared between her thighs, and on her breasts were the two words – 'Mild' – 'Bitter'.

There was still no movement from the door. Placing one hand on its centre, Jock pushed slightly and it sprang open. This second room was, if anything, even more unwholesome than the first. The bed appeared to consist of nothing more than a pile of grimy, grey blankets. The torch beam explored the room. There was a wardrobe, two chairs and a bucket, but the only sign of Freda and her 'fiancé' was an assorted pile of clothing on the floor.

Gladys pushed forward between us like some great whale. She reached on to the bed and with one grand and powerful sweep yanked back the blankets. There, locked in each other's arms, lay the babes in the wood, or rather Freda and her Joe. My first reaction was they were midgets. They were so tangled together that it would have been impossible to tell where one stopped and the other began, except that he was black and she was white.

Freda was so slight she was almost boyish. In fact, in comparison to Gladys she was practically invisible. Her partner was only slightly larger. It was very obvious why the foursome had paired off as they had. Both occupants of the bed were awake. He was all eyes, which were rolling around in obvious terror, while Freda was attempting to hide, by burying into him.

'Get up, lovelies, it's the law,' said Gladys.

The relief on the face of Freda's fiancé was instant. He'd obviously assumed he was about to be the victim of a set-up. He was either going to be 'rolled' for his cash or, equally dubiously, approached by an outraged 'husband'. Either way it was going to be expensive.

If I'd had any lingering doubts as to whether these last few minutes had been the least erotic of my entire life, the question was finally determined by Gladys's next action. Toddling across to the bucket that stood in the corner of the room, she squatted astride it and calmly, but loudly, cascaded into it for almost a full minute.

'I 'ave trouble with me water-works, lovely,' she smiled, by way of explanation.

We were joined by 'Choc'y' who was now fully dressed and in fact looked quite smart.

'C'mon,' said Jock, 'it's aboot teem we all adjourned to the station.'

The journey from the house to the Old Kent Road was, by and large, uneventful. That is, if one disregards Gladys's attempts to negotiate the window sill in an extremely tight pencil skirt. The cleaners and market workers who gathered at the bus-stops looked on in amazement as our strange entourage threaded its way between them. Freda and Joe resembled two famine-racked ballet-dancers, while Choc'y and Gladys could have been contenders for the world heavy-weight crown. The group was sternly led by Jock, pushing his still creaking bike, his old cycle clips reflecting the first rays of the early morning sun; and I fetched up the rear.

Gladys chattered incessantly, mainly to Choc'y. He responded merely by the odd grunt, or occasional nod. Freda huddled close into Joe and the pair walked along in total silence. Some twenty minutes later, the police van had deposited us all at Wharf Road and the seven of us, plus the station officer, held a discussion in the interview room.

Both girls, it seemed, had worked in the past for Jolly John, although, surprisingly, they appeared to have no previous convictions. They had obviously picked up the two airmen and, in the absence of a car or any other accommodation, decided to return to 110a. Their story of an engagement was a shrewd idea of Gladys's. No vice law ever prevented fiancés sharing a bed, even if it did seem to be inside a brothel. The whole episode appeared to be little more than a case of trespassing and there was no way that Jolly John would have prosecuted for that.

Both men were in possession of Air Base passes that had expired more than a week earlier. It was decided to inform the USAF at Bushey Park of their whereabouts and leave any action concerning them to the American authorities. They were then shown into the interview room and given a cup of tea. The girls, subject to no stolen property being found on them, would be released and Jolly John would be notified.

Surprisingly quickly, an enclosed USAF truck arrived outside the front entrance of Wharf Road. The vehicle rocked from side to side as four of the largest men that I had ever seen alighted. Two were black, one was white, while the last was rather Greek in appearance. I did not know their ranks – I've never really come to terms with the structure in my own force – but they had stripes and ribbons almost everywhere.

''Mornin', sur,' said the Greek, with extreme politeness. 'I'm Sergeant Atropus, these here are my men. You'se have two of our guys here, I believe, sur?'

'Yes,' I replied, 'they're having a cup of tea in the interview room.'

'Do I sign for them, sur?'

'No, they have not been charged. Simply collect them.'

'Thank you, sur.'

I led all four men into the small room where Choc'y and Joe sat quietly sipping tea. It was very obvious by the pair's reaction that they had not expected their escorts quite so soon. They both dropped their cups and simultaneously made a rush for the door. They hadn't a snowball in hell's chance of making it, guarded as it was by the four giants. Each of these escorts dropped instantly on to the luckless pair and after the briefest of struggles, both men were bundled into the truck.

'Thank you for yo' co-operation, sur,' said Sergeant Atropus.

'Any time. Incidentally, besides being absent, are those two lads wanted for anything else?'

'They sure are, sur, they sure are! These are just two almighty bad guys, sur – two almighty bad guys!'

The truck then roared off, leaving me none the wiser and with a feeling that I had been somehow used.

I returned to the interview room to find that Gladys and Freda had, under Jock Tiffleck's somewhat gruff instructions, tipped their handbags on to the table and scattered the contents. At first glance there appeared to be little to distinguish them from the contents of any other young ladies' handbags. That is, with the exception of two small packets that remained in a fastened fold in Gladys's bag. The first packet, not surprisingly, contained three contraceptives. The second was far more puzzling. After undoing several layers of tissue, I finally came to a small wad, neatly wrapped in a cigarette paper. I carefully rolled back the final cover and was surprised to find the 'wad' consisted entirely of curly, fine hairs, some two inches in length and rather pleasantly perfumed.

The perfume was so fragrant that I raised the package to my face and sniffed deeply.

'This smells really nice. What is it?' I asked.

'My pewbs, lovely,' replied Gladys, matter-of-factly.

'Your what?'

'My pewbs – my pubic hairs,' she explained.

I dropped them instantly. The memory of her enormous bulk squatting over that bucket was altogether too fresh in my mind.

'Ugh!! What the hell do you do with them?' I shuddered.

'I sell them to clients, lovely.'

'Well, what do they do with them?'

Jock Tiffleck could obviously stand no more. Striding

over to the table, he picked up the entire contents in one huge fist and thrust them back into her handbag.

'They grind 'em doone, laddie – and then they use 'em fur snuff!' he roared.

I spent the next fifteen minutes in the surgeon's room, scrubbing my nails until they almost bled.

Later that morning, as I wearily inserted my key in my front door, the exhaustion I had felt in the early part of the night returned. I staggered up the steps and, within a few minutes, had collapsed on to the bed. Usually, on returning home after night-duty I provided my wife Joan with a cup of tea before she arose for work. This day I was much too tired.

'You all right?' she asked sleepily.

I grunted some sort of acknowledgement.

'Why are you so tired?' she persisted.

'I spent the night in a brothel.'

'Oh,' she said. 'I'll make my own tea, then.'

A Few Irish Parties

The piano accordion could be heard fully 200 yards away from the King's Head public house. It seemed to thrive on the competition offered by the Gaelic oaths and breaking glass. The soft strains of 'The Londonderry Air' had certainly had to struggle when hostilities first commenced, but now that the accordionist had switched to 'It's Christmas in Killarney', he had taken an unassailable lead.

In the normal course of events, the King's Head was a very well run pub, but within the last few months it had slipped sadly downhill. This was not altogether surprising. Danny Coyle, the rotund licensee, had run his pub with a firm hand. The 'hand' actually belonged to his firm wife Doris. Doris, in turn, had not only run the pub but had now run away – with the piano player twenty years her junior.

Since Doris's departure, Danny had found a very remunerative way of supplementing his income. He had gone into Saturday wedding receptions in a big way. These weddings, usually Irish, were slowly losing Danny all the local goodwill built up by Doris over the last fifteen years. Doris had had no illusions – or scruples. She had willingly catered for a largely Irish clientele in both saloon and public bars. She had, however, always refused to hire out the large room above the pub for weddings.

'Too much bloody aggro, weddings,' she'd always said.

Doris most certainly had a point. Since Danny had entered the field of matrimonial catering, the police had been called to almost every alternate wedding above the pub. Matters were going to look pretty black for poor old Danny at the annual licensing sessions.

We were well short of men that July afternoon and I wasn't overthrilled about attending a riotous Irish wedding on my own. On the other hand I had always found the Irish to be great respecters of uniform, so perhaps, not for the first time, the navy-blue serge would see me through.

Danny Coyle met me at the saloon-bar door.

'It's der bride's family. Der's apparently an uncle who's caused all der grief and oi'd like him out.'

'You know, you're fast becoming a real right pain in the arse, Dan. It's almost every week now that we have this problem.'

'Oi can't help it if dey fight can oi? Oi don't go up der and tell 'em to start, do oi?'

'All I know is, Dan, that no other pub in the area collects the same amount of trouble that you seem to.'

'Whell if it gets too bad, oi've always got der "kennedy" under der bar.'

Dan's 'kennedy' was a large wooden cosh that he kept handy in case of emergencies. There had been at least two occasions when injuries sustained in his pub had been consistent with a wallop from the 'kennedy'. So far, though, no one had complained of either seeing it in anger, or feeling it, in even greater anger.

'Well, I think "kennedy" could stay indoors today. You might stick close to the phone, though, just in case I need some assistance.'

'Dat I whill do,' replied Dan enthusiastically.

'Firstly, though, if you want anyone "put outside", you'll have to ask them in my presence to leave. All I can do is to offer assistance if you are unable to cope, understand?'

Dan understood right enough, he'd had it explained to

him more times than all the other Wharf Road publicans put together.

'Sure, but oi still tink dat dis is a good toime to get der "kennedy" out.'

'Dan, for Christ's sake! Will you forget the bloody "kennedy"?'

He nodded reluctantly.

Together we began to climb the steps that led up to the reception room. The stairs reminded me of the Grand Rapids. Beer was cascading down each of them like a series of small waterfalls. The volume of noise was already falling when I pushed open the door and looked into the crowded room. Lying out cold at my feet was the man whom I soon discovered to be the infamous uncle of the bride. His unconscious state was almost certainly connected with the lump at the rear of his ear. This lump, in its turn, had more than a passing connection with the broken chair lying all around him. Surprising, though, as this sight was, it was nothing to the sight on the far wall. Two-thirds of the way up the wallpaper, and probably only held in place by a double-unit wall lamp was the wedding cake! It was slowly beginning to travel down the wall.

Eamon (the sleeping uncle) had apparently been responsible for that particular piece of decor. It had been the final straw for the bride's father, a man small of stature and large of temper. As the cake had struck the wall so the chair had struck Eamon. Both sides of the dispute agreed that this was a very fair exchange and honours now appeared to be even. So far, almost so good. The fight had ended, the accordionist had switched back to a more mellowing tune, and no one had actually lost face. Except, that is, for Eamon: he had almost lost a head.

'Before I sort this bloke out, Dan,' I said pointing to the recumbent Eamon, 'what are your feelings about the situation?'

'Whell, dere's nothin' dere for me to worry about now.

Joust a few broken glasses and a cake-stain on der wall. Dat'll soon wash off. No, oi'm quite happy,' he answered cheerfully.

'You know, I somehow thought you might be,' I said, kneeling down beside the now wakening figure on the floor. 'Are you all right, Paddy?' I asked, rather caringly, I thought.

'Fooking hell, sur! There was no need to hit me loike dat, sur,' he gasped, rubbing the back of his head vigorously.

'I didn't do it! Although I understand one of your family may know something about it.'

'Dat's all right, sur. I know you have your job to do and p'raps I was a little boisterous, sur.'

'I tell you, I didn't bloody do it! I wasn't even in the room. In any case, I wouldn't have hit you with a chair. Haven't you got any recollection about it at all?'

'Oh yes, sur. Oi remember now, sur. I was dancing and I slipped, sur. Slipped over backwards oi did and banged me head, sur. Sure it's nothing really.' He again frantically rubbed the base of his skull.

'I think you ought to go to hospital for an X-ray at the very least. After all, you've been unconscious for a couple of minutes.'

'No, sur, oi'm foine, sur, really oi am.'

'Are you sure?'

'Certainly, sur.'

'Did anyone see what happened?' I optimistically asked the room in general.

Only two people spoke; they were brothers of Eamon. They both agreed he was indeed dancing and fell over backwards and banged his head. The bride's father, who bore an uncanny resemblance to Stan Laurel, blinked his eyes and scratched his head. The two brothers then lifted Eamon to a chair and thrust a pint of Guinness into his huge fist. His feet were already moving in time to the accordionist, so at least his responses looked okay.

'Well, I'm wasting my time here,' I said to Dan. 'I'll report the incident at Wharf Road nick on my return.'

'Whill you have a drink, officer?'

I was sorely tempted, but Eamon was yet to be convinced that it wasn't me who had all but brained him with the chair. I looked at him again; he was rapidly gaining strength through his Guinness. I thought perhaps now would be a prudent time to leave. On my way down the staircase, it suddenly occurred to me that at no time had I seen either the bride or the groom. I had supposed there was such a couple – but you can never be really sure at an Irish wedding.

I had hoped I had seen the last of Eamon, and so it was – well, at least for another four years. Then one spring Sunday afternoon I was driving the area car (Mike 3) with a young wireless operator, John Quiller, in his very first posting on the car. Our first call was to number 186 The Albany. This location was an old tenement block about half a mile from the station. The phantom bride and groom whom I had never actually seen those four years ago had had an addition to their family, and a Christening party had been arranged. With the self-flagellation that so many Irish families practise, Eamon had been not only forgiven – but invited! At first I did not recognize him. A serious illness, from which he had completely recovered, had resulted in the loss of all his body hair. This made him appear, if anything, an even more daunting figure.

The call had been to the Christening lunch. Twenty people were sitting down to eat, in a flat that must have been claustrophobic with four kids and a goldfish. I never did make it inside the flat. We had been called by a neighbour complaining about the noise, but the place was fairly quiet on our arrival. Eamon appeared at the door but, thankfully, he failed to recognize me from the wedding. Behind him, looking more like Stan Laurel than ever, was the bride's father. I thought, 'If you knew what I knew, mate, you'd never turn your back on him, particularly if there is a chair about.' Everyone was surprisingly sober, and after pointing out that some neighbours were a little concerned at the noise, I left the premises. I felt deep down, however, that we would be back. I just could not see a dish with all those ingredients fail to come to the boil. At the next eruption, three hours later, we were at the other end of the manor and already dealing with a slight traffic accident. The disturbance was therefore taken by two foot PCs from Wharf Road. We could scarcely believe our good fortune. This wasn't to last, however.

Some time later, having finished our cooked tea and written up our accident report, John and I were ready for the second half of our stint. I slipped the car into first gear and the big old Wolseley saloon rolled quietly out into the Walworth Road. Or rather, that is what should have happened. It was unable to do so on this occasion, because the far side of the Walworth Road was absolutely solid with traffic.

'Quarter to eight on a Sunday evening and a traffic jam in Walworth Road?' queried a puzzled John.

'Another bloody accident, I suppose. I hate Sunday drivers,' I answered piously.

Northbound traffic was flowing freely enough, but southbound was not moving at all. A small, northbound Fiat skidded to a halt across my bows, the driver leapt out and he ran over to my open window.

There's a terrible fight down there, guv'nor!' he said. 'It's all over the pavement, that's why the traffic's not moving. They're all sitting in their cars watching it!'

I switched on the flashing blue light and took to the offside of the two idling lanes of southbound traffic. A quarter of a mile down the road was the Fountain public house. Outside these premises was obviously one hell of a commotion. We could not actually see what form it was taking, because our view was restricted by the two stationary lines of traffic on our nearside. I slowly edged the area car to the kerbside and John and I leapt out. We saw a group of about ten people on the pavement. They all seemed intent on doing a serious mischief to a huge bald fellow in their midst.

'He looks like the "Last of the Mohicans",' exclaimed John.

I had to admit that for the first time Eamon looked more sinned against than sinning. On the cry: 'It's der poe-lease', everyone except Eamon scattered in a dozen different directions. Pursuit was pointless for they were all Eamon's relations and could be picked up later should the need arise.

Eamon, not yet aware of our presence, was still yelling to his assailants to come back and fight. He was bleeding profusely from numerous small cuts and abrasions but, on the whole, did not appear too badly hurt. Arriving from behind him, I foolishly took hold of his massive forearm in an effort to calm him down. Roaring loudly, he seized hold of my wrists and spun around and away from me. He pivoted on one foot and we both fell to the ground – with me underneath.

Almost immediately, and before John could dive in and rescue me, Eamon realized his mistake. His mood changed instantly. He was at least three-quarters drunk and there is no creature in the world more attentive than a well-meaning drunk. With one powerful movement of his arms, he jerked me to my feet and apologized to excess.

'Jesus, Mary and Joseph! Oi'm sorry, sur, oi'm sorry. It was dat bunch, sur. Dey's der one's. Dey made me foight. Oi didn't know it was you, sur, dat oi didn't. Oi'm sorry, sur.'

With that he proceeded to brush me down with two huge hands.

It was not until that precise moment that I had noticed his breath. I assumed this was because it was the first time we had been in such close proximity. I wondered what illness he had suffered from. Perhaps even still suffering from. Whatever it was, it was also the very last word in halitosis. Each breath he released seemed to assail not just my nostrils, but my lungs and my eyes. It was so strong I felt I could almost see it. If I had reached out I was sure I could have touched it. The smell travelled down my throat and spread through my upper respiratory tract. It was so overpowering that I turned my head.

'Oi'm sorry, sur, oi'm sorry,' he kept repeating.

'It's all right, Eamon, it's all right,' I repeated back.

I then needed to summon up all my courage to ask him the usual 'common assault' questions.

'Are you okay? Do you wish to go to hospital? Do you know your assailants? If so, do you wish any action taken against them?'

'No, sur! Dey meant no harm, sur.'

While he was talking, I'd been walking backwards around the front of the parked police car. John had already shrewdly slid into the R/T operator's seat. My problem was much greater: not only was I walking backwards but I had to open the driver's door against a stream of fast-moving traffic.

Eamon gave me my last brush down and, once he was sure I was in the vehicle, slammed the door shut. I could hardly believe my ordeal was over. I imagined I could still smell him.

I turned to John and said, 'That man must have only hours to live. He's got the worst breath of anyone I ever smelt in my life!'

'You've got dog-shit in your whistle chain,' said John quietly, as he rolled down the window.

I looked down at my tunic. There, beneath my chin, was the chrome chain that ran between my left breast-pocket and my first buttonhole. It was festooned with faeces and it was wafting some six inches beneath my nostrils.

Poor Eamon! Not only was he innocent of all that I had credited him with, but he was probably thinking the same evil-smelling thoughts about me!

It would be misleading to give the impression that the social role of members of the police force is simply to act as referees at drinking parties. Not so. Some of the liveliest parties that I have ever been to have been held by and for policemen. All, I hasten to say, in their off-duty capacity. (With the possible exception of one constable who, just before he was sacked, rode his police motorcycle in through one door of a saloon bar and out through the other.)

I was looking forward to attending one such party on a warm summer Saturday a few years ago. On the day in question, however, I was posted late-turn area car driver with my friend Bootsie Hill, who was the radio operator. Bootsie and I had a problem. We had spent half the previous week trying to arrange a change of leave but no matter how we wriggled we had been unsuccessful. It was the height of the holiday period and we were both stuck with our least favourite duty, 3 p.m. to 11 p.m. on a Saturday. The irony was that the party was being held by Bootsie's new girl-friend. We had come to terms with the fact that we were not going to be able to change our leaves. All we could hope for was that we at least finished on time. Even this was no easy task, particularly on long hot summer weekends.

The tantalizing aspect about that whole day was that it was just about the quietest Saturday that I had ever spent in the force. As the clock hands moved slowly nearer eleven o'clock, I became more and more restless. I felt it just could not last. It didn't.

At 10.30 p.m., just as the car was practically pointing its

own nose in the direction of the station, we received our first call of the day.

'Mike 3. Peckham Road junction Benhill Road. Serious racial disturbance!'

'Well, isn't that just bloody marvellous?' I cursed, as I turned the car reluctantly around and switched on the blue lamp.

'If we're going to have a call, we may as well have a big 'un,' said Bootsie resignedly.

'It's going to be a three-o'clock-in-the-morning finish. I just know it is,' I groaned pessimistically.

Our noisy arrival at the scene, with our klaxon sounding, car horn hooting and all lights blazing, was fairly rapid, for we had been no more than half a mile away when we received the call. I was appalled at the sight that greeted us. There must have been fifty people scattered all over the road, furiously fighting each other. Half of them were white, the remainder black. Another hundred or so were watching the combatants and offering encouragement. The traffic was at a complete standstill and three cars occupied the centre of the carriageway, where they had shunted into each other. It looked a very good time to call for assistance.

As far as I was ever able to ascertain, the cause of the fracas was the three-vehicle accident. The front vehicle had stopped fairly suddenly in the centre of the road, waiting to turn right. The second car had stopped just inches short of it. The third car had run into the back of the second car, nudging it into the rear of the first. The first vehicle had contained five Irishmen on their way to a wedding party in a house in the sidestreet. The second and third cars contained several West Indians, all close friends of each other. Both West Indian drivers had then left their vehicles and remonstrated with the Irish driver for stopping so suddenly. The occupants of all three cars then happily joined in, together with several black passers-by and about twenty revellers from the Irish party.

The crowd thinned rapidly as the first of our assistance arrived. The milling throng had been so great, it had been impossible to tell who was a combatant and who was a spectator. A determined threat to nick anyone still on the scene after a ten-second count had the desired effect of clearing away most people, except the three cars and their occupants. None of the injured wished to involve the police and while all three drivers certainly appeared to have been drinking, each was far from the breathalyzing limit. Even the damage to the vehicles was slight, the rear bumper of the second car being the main casualty. No offence was apparent from a quick examination of all three vehicles, and each driver was quite happy to exchange names and addresses. Soon, all that was left at the scene was Bootsie and I, plus a broken car bumper.

'Well, we've done it, son!' I was just about to utter, when a black couple approached me.

'My wife's having a miscarriage as a result of watching that most distressing experience,' he complained.

I quickly examined her while Bootsie called an ambulance. She was truly enormous and her thighs were soaked. I attempted to sit her on the front passenger seat of the police car but there was simply no room for her vast bulk. Bootsie and I then swung her legs around and placed her feet on the pavement.

'I think we ought to lay her down,' whispered Bootsie.

'Well, it would have to be across the car seats, then we'd never manage to get her up again!' I protested.

Our deliberations were soon cut short by the far off sound of a two-tone horn. In the distance, swerving in and out of the now free-flowing traffic, the comforting sight of a London ambulance came into view. I am always impressed by the unruffled professionalism of ambulance crews.

'Wotcha got, mate?' called the driver cheerfully as he alighted from his cabin.

I gave a brief explanation and very gently the two crew-men escorted the lady the few yards into the rear of the ambulance. Pulling the doors partially closed behind them, they carried out a cursory examination.

Two minutes later, we were astonished to see the doors of the ambulance open wide and both husband and wife emerge. She stepped boldly down the two steps and they strode quickly away towards Camberwell. Both crew-men looked slightly amused as they closed the rear doors of the ambulance and moved off towards the front of their vehicle.

'Nothing to worry about there, mate,' called one of them.

'What happened?' I said anxiously.

'She'd wet her knickers!' he laughed, and they sped rapidly off towards King's College Hospital. Bootsie and I watched as the ambulance faded into the distance.

'I think we're out of the wood, Boots,' I said, perhaps a trifle prematurely.

Bootsie nodded and raised his eyes.

''Ere, I fink that's real dangerous, that is,' said an old cockney voice.

I turned to see an elderly man standing behind me.

'What is?' I snapped irritably, suddenly being aware of a little more of the wood than I'd expected.

'That car bumper laying in the gutter, that's wot is.'

'Well, it's broken and it's useless,' explained Bootsie.

'Still didn't orta be there, though, did it?' said our street lawyer.

'I'll tell you what,' confided Bootsie. 'I'll appoint you solely responsible for getting rid of it. All right?'

'All right,' responded the old fellow.

Leaving our latest acquaintance to his specially allocated task, we two hastened back towards our car. We settled ourselves, I reversed from the main road into the sidestreet, and I was just about to engage first gear when suddenly an almighty crash of breaking glass rent the late evening air.

'Christ Almighty! What now?'

I nosed the car forward so we could just see around the corner. The only person in sight was our street lawyer; of the car bumper, there was no sign. I turned the car into the main road and within seconds we drew alongside the old fellow.

'Where's the car bumper?'

'Gorn.'

'Gorn where?'

'Over the wall.'

'What d'you mean, over the wall?'

'I frew-it-over-the-wall,' he said, emphasizing every syllable as if he were talking to a deaf foreigner.

'But there's the vicar's greenhouse over the wall!' said Bootsie.

'Dunno nuffink abaht that. You told me to get rid of it, didn't cha?'

'Boots,' I said, 'it's party time.'

'You're right,' answered Bootsie, looking at his watch. 'It's exactly eleven o'clock.'

Sunday, Boring Sunday

The deep-throated bark of next door's dog lifted me through those last layers of sleep. Each morning, as regular as clockwork, the paper boy calls. Also each morning, equally regular, the stupid dog reacts as if the Cossacks are rampaging down the street. I reluctantly emerged into the half-light world of a grey November Sunday. The rain streamed steadily down the window-panes and poured relentlessly into the gutterings. I sat up in bed and peered through the gap in the curtains. Rolls and rolls of buffeting grey clouds stretched away over the cemetery. God! It must be raining across the whole world.

Suddenly I remembered, I was on duty that afternoon from 4 p.m. till midnight! Ugh, what a prospect! I studied the sky again. One did not have to be a meteorologist to realize that it was going to rain not just all day but tomorrow as well. It may even rain forever – it looked that sort of rain.

Besides the rain, I had an additional problem. My car was sick. It was in the local garage with a serious, and so far undiagnosed, ailment. I was relying on a colleague, who lived close by and worked at a neighbouring station, for a lift. He was due to begin work at 4 p.m.; I had therefore changed my own duty time to correspond with his. 'Four till midnight', on a cold wet November Sunday, was not a duty that I would choose lightly.

Around 3.30 p.m., a gentle toot-toot indicated that my chauffeur had arrived. Still tying my tie, I ran down the garden path and climbed into his car.

'How about your raincoat?' called my wife.

I airily waved away any suggestion of it. His car was warm, it was reliable, and he was picking me up from my own station at midnight. What did I need a raincoat for?

Some thirty minutes later, well wrapped up in my uniform great-coat, I booked on at the Wharf Road duty-slate. I was pleasantly surprised to see my colleague Dave Biss, who was starting duty at the same time. Dave and I were good friends and also community coppers in adjoining beats. We shared many off-duty interests, the most passionate of these being wildlife conservation, particularly of whales. Well, with any luck we would walk around today and put a few of the ecology problems of the world to rights. We left the station and walked slowly along the Walworth Road. The rain continued unabated.

'I hate late turn Sundays,' I said to Dave. 'They are just so bloody boring.'

An ambulance raced by on its way to an accident at Camberwell Green.

'Even the emergency calls are predictable,' agreed Dave.

Our conversation was interrupted for a while. The rain had triggered off several Walworth Road burglar alarms, but many of these shop-owners were away for the day and could not be contacted.

On a muddy building site, half a mile away, two twelve-year-old kids who could scarcely write their own names were about to start the engine of a sophisticated £15,000 earth remover. Here, within the next twenty minutes, they would demolish six weeks' work of three skilled bricklayers.

'If every day was as boring as Sundays are I'd leave the job tomorrow,' I responded.

In a nearby block of flats Jack Egan struck his wife Rose

a shuddering blow across her mouth. Ten minutes later Rose left him, for the fourth time that year.

'It's the rain that does it, you know. The manor just dies on a wet Sunday.'

The drunks and vagrants in the derelict houses reshuffled their ragged bedding to avoid the constant drips from the gaping roof.

'I admit it *is* strange how nothing seems to happen on a Sunday.'

On the fifteenth floor of Bateman House, Mary Taylor was painfully giving birth to her third. While opposite, at the Braganza Old People's Home, ninety-six-year-old Nellie Nettleton, the home's oldest inhabitant, simply stopped breathing.

'There's hardly a soul about.'

Twelve-year-old Dean Shorewell, with his head reeling and stomach heaving, took yet another deep drag on his cigarette and convinced himself he looked at least twenty years old.

Dave and I agreed – Sundays were just one big bore.

Suddenly our personal radios croaked into life.

'604 and 222 [Dave and I] return to Wharf Road as soon as possible.'

I acknowledged the call and could not resist asking, 'Why?'

'Don't be a nosy sod,' came back the rather unprofessional reply.

We turned around into the wind, the cold rain stinging our faces.

'Whatever it is, I don't want to walk very far in this weather,' said Dave, burying his chin in his coat collar.

Some ten minutes later, we entered the front office where Sergeant Cage sat deceptively quiet behind a typewriter.

'D'you want us, sergeant?' I asked.

'Ah yes! Our intrepid explorers!'

Dave and I just looked blank.

'Because of your love of wildlife, I'm going to send you two on a voyage of discovery. How about that?'

'Are you telling me that you are doing me a favour, sergeant?' I asked suspiciously.

'Of course.'

'Then we don't want to go – wherever it is. It's quite all right, sergeant, we'll go for a long walk in the freezing rain. We may even tackle three armed gunmen, or perhaps a mentally deranged gang armed with meat cleavers. Perhaps we'll scale a skyscraper block from the outside. I know! A rabid dog! Perhaps we'll deal with that. You do have a rabid dog, don't you, sergeant?'

'Or even a bear!' broke in Dave.

'Yes, even a bear, or perhaps a bear and a dog,' I agreed. 'In fact anything at all in preference to one of your bloody favours. I've had some – and I don't like 'em. They've lost their magic for me!'

'Boys, boys,' he responded in a hurt tone. 'Look, see this simple piece of paper?' He leaned forward across the desk and, picking up a small form, waved it gently across our faces. 'This piece of paper is really magic. It's going to open up whole new horizons for you. You'll meet lots of fascinating new people, you'll have your mind broadened, you'll travel, you'll . . .'

'Travel?!!!'

'Yes, "travel". This simple paper is in reality a travel warrant. It is a warrant to the one place in the country that I am prepared to bet neither of you have been. Yet it is one place that you have always wished to go! They are, in fact, one and the same! I am going to do you both a favour. I am assisting you two to fulfil a lifetime's ambition.'

'Where's that warrant made out to?' demanded Dave.

'Wigan,' said Sergeant Cage, with the air of a man who really enjoys keeping his trump card to the very last.

'Wigan? Where the hell is Wigan?' I groaned.

'You'll like it – it's very nice there,' he beamed.

Now was the time for the counter-attack, but he had his defences well marshalled, he parried every question skilfully.

'I've got no car,' I thrust.

'I've got no coat,' said Dave.

'Neither have I,' I echoed.

'We're not dressed for it. We've only got our uniform coats here.' (More or less both together.)

'We're off duty at midnight,' pleaded Dave.

'I don't know where Wigan is! I don't speak Wigan! And I don't wish to go there!'

'Well, today, then, is a big day in your life. You are going to go to Wigan; you're going to meet a Wiganer and you're going to really enjoy it,' stated Peter Cage, with the satisfaction of one who fully realizes when he has won an argument.

'Give us the details, then,' I said, with the resignation of one who equally realizes when he has lost.

'There's a train just before 6 p.m. from Euston. The Wigan police will meet you at the railway station and hand over to you a car thief named Elvis Presley Clements. Young Elvis is wanted at this station for about six thefts of motor vehicles. A train returns from Wigan for Euston about ten minutes after you arrive there. You'll be back in London about 11.45 p.m. and you'll be no more than ten minutes late booking off. How's that?'

'How's that?' I echoed. 'I don't believe it, that's "how's that". In the first place, no escort that I have ever been on is as simple as that. In the second place – well, ask yourself. If someone told you to go to Wigan to collect Elvis Presley for nicking a car, what would your reaction be?'

'Look! You haven't got time to argue. Put on your civvy jacket, the van is waiting outside to take you to Euston and you've got something like thirty minutes to catch your train. Now 'op it!'

So saying, he resumed his typing, although he could not completely hide his smile of delight.

Police vans are not the most luxurious of vehicles, and the gales that buffeted the side of the van fostered countless draughts. This proved to be a fair indication of what the elements had in store for us. The van driver arrived at Euston with barely minutes to spare. We changed our warrant for a ticket at the booking office, and ran through the barrier to the waiting train. Almost as an afterthought I doubled back to the ticket collector.

'Do we have to change for Wigan, please?' I asked.

He fumbled in his waistcoat pocket and removed from it a battered old card. He studied it while Dave sighed impatiently.

'Change at Crewe,' he stated officially.

Dave and I resumed our run.

'Just as well I asked him,' I panted, a trifle smugly. 'We'd have been on the wrong train otherwise.'

We settled in the corner seat of a long carriage. Our only reading matter was two tea-stained morning papers, snatched quickly from our station canteen. I began to study our fellow passengers. I was surprised how many there were. For some reason I thought we would be the only passengers. I could not imagine who would wish to travel up to the north-west corner of the country on such a wild bleak day.

About two and a half hours later, the diesel throbbed its way into Crewe Station. Leaving our newspapers on the train, we each yawned, stretched and alighted. The first change we noticed was the temperature. It had been cold in London but the wind was absolutely cutting up here. Being coatless, we did not wish to stand around too long. I saw a uniformed railway inspector close by and, striding briskly up to him, I asked the time of the next train to Wigan.

'Tha's joust got off of eet,' he said matter-of-factly.

'Tha'll be anuther in a coople o' 'ours' teem, though.'

'You mean that train goes to Wigan?' I asked incredulously. (It had now just left the platform.)

'Aye.'

'But the ticket collector at Euston told us we had to change! We've got other connections to make,' I wailed.

'Tha doan't wanta believe all tha tells tha in London. They know nowt down ther. The'er all daft.'

'You're bloody right about that. If he's collecting tickets when we return, I'll stuff 'em up him!'

'Who's the clever-dick who asked if he had to change trains,' said Dave, with only slight bitterness in his voice.

We now had two long hours to look around Crewe Station. That operation can be completed sufficiently in thirty-eight seconds. When the end of the world arrives, it will take only second place to Crewe on a bleak November Sunday. We sat on a post office mail-bag trolley for a while, then Dave found the station waiting room. A few minutes in the waiting room sent us hurrying back to the trolley. Wherever we hid, the wind sought us out. No matter which corner, corridor or doorway, it cut gleefully down our collars and up our sleeves. The time dragged, each minute colder and longer than the previous one. All the time I kept thinking that we were once on the right bloody train! If I killed that ticket collector, would it be justifiable homicide? No jury would ever convict me, certainly no jury that had ever changed at Crewe. After what seemed a year, another diesel vibrated alongside our platform. Three-quarters of an hour later, we were in Wigan.

For some reason, every time I went to the music-hall when I was a kid, there would be a comic who would make a derisory remark about Wigan. I will never know if he told the truth, because all we saw was the rain. It billowed and swept all before it. All I discovered in Wigan were fourteen people who did not know where the police station was. I spoke to each of them individually within five minutes of leaving the train.

'Per-lease Sta-shun? Nay, but tha knows summat? It's round 'ere somewhere.'

We ran, heads down, first in one direction then in another. Swinging shop and pub signs would gather the pouring rain and then deposit it on the two scurrying, coatless figures underneath. Eventually we staggered, ice-cold and saturated, into the enquiry room in Wigan Police Station. God knows what we looked like, but an enormous sergeant at first refused to believe our story.

Once they ascertained we were not mental escapees, they made us quite welcome. First though, we both needed to telephone home. It was now about fifteen minutes after midnight. The amount of time I waited for an answer told me that my wife Joan had already retired to bed.

'Er – I'll be home a bit late, luv. I'm in Wigan!'

'Wigan! But you haven't got a raincoat!'

'I *know* I haven't got a raincoat,' I replied tersely. 'In fact, it would be true to say that if there is one thing in the whole world of which I am really sure, it is that I haven't got a raincoat!'

'When will you be home?'

'Well, I should have been in London half an hour ago. If I receive the same help from British Rail on my return as I received coming up, then I'll be back about Thursday. Otherwise it will be some time tomorrow.'

A quick glance at Dave told me his conversation was much the same as mine. We rang off and looked for food.

About an hour later, having partially thawed out, we began to make enquiries about our prisoner. The next train for London was not due till 3.30 a.m., when a police car would run the three of us to the railway station. Elvis was a fairly inoffensive bloke – providing it wasn't your car he was nicking – and at this precise moment he was sensibly fast asleep. Whether it was the lateness of the hour or the police station acoustics that was responsible, I don't really know, but both Dave and I had great difficulty in understanding the sergeant's accent. So many times we answered his queries with 'Pardon?' that we both began to *guess* what he said.

'Have ye nae coo'se?' he called across the counter to Dave. At least I thought that was what he called.

'Er – pardon?'

'Coo'se, Coo'se! Have ye nae coo'se?' He was becoming quite irritable with Dave's apparent deafness.

'He means "coats",' I whispered side-mouthed to Dave.

'No, sergeant,' answered Dave, pleased enough at last to be able to answer a question. 'You see, we didn't expect to come up here. We could have really done with them, though, whilst we were running around Crewe. They might at least have kept the rain off – and the cold out.'

'Keep bloody re-ain off?? Keep bloody cold oot?? What wi'? These bloody things?'

So saying, he picked up a pair of handcuffs from his desk and jangled them in front of Dave. I just looked away and pretended it was nothing to do with me. What had sounded like 'coo'se' to me had been 'cuffs' to the sergeant. It didn't matter anyway, we had neither coats, coo'se nor cuffs!

'Ye understand that when tha signs for 'im, he's tha responsibility?'

'Yes, sergeant,' Dave acknowledged.

We both dozed for a few minutes in a couple of canteen chairs. We were soon awakened by a young giant of a PC who offered a cup of tea and a friendly grin.

'Tha sergeant thinks tha bloody useless,' he chuckled. 'He reckons tha'll lose Elvis afore tha gets ta Crewe.'

Dave and I responded with two very tight smiles.

'Anyway, drink oop, train's due in fifteen minutes. Ma name's Joe.'

Five minutes later, with Dave and Joe in the front of the police car, I was handcuffed to Elvis in the back. Joe parked the vehicle in the station forecourt and, fighting the gale all the way, we struggled along the platform to the waiting room. Dave opened the door and I was amazed at the sight that greeted us. The room looked like a set from an old pre-war Will Hay film. The six characters, who were sleeping in various poses, all reinforced this impression. Just inside the door was a wooden table which Joe sat on while he undid the cuffs. These cuffs were the property of the Wigan police and as such they could not leave with Elvis. We now had to be alert all the way back to London.

The crash must have almost been heard back at the police station. Poor Elvis jumped almost out of his skin. One of the legs of the table had given way and Joe disappeared backwards over the table. Only two of the sleeping inhabitants even stirred! In our concern for poor Joe, Dave and I completely forgot Elvis. We were quite relieved to see him sitting on the bench, near the ashes of the long-dead fire.

'Due to storm damage, we regret to announce the delay of the London-bound train on Platform 2. There is an indefinite delay but it is expected to be no longer than one hour.'

'Right – cuffs on, Elvis,' said Joe, now recovered from his tumble. 'We'll go back to station an' wait.'

I glanced around the room as we left. No one else had even stirred!

Joe arranged with the railway staff that they would telephone the police station when the train left Preston, a few miles up the line.

'I don't think we are ever going to return to London somehow,' said Elvis gloomily.

'It's your bloody fault if we don't. If you had kept your hands off other people's cars we wouldn't all be sodding about here in the middle of the bloody night.' I glowered.

'It'd serve you right if they gave you the bill for this little lot – including the table!'

The thought of being presented with the bill quite distressed Elvis. He retreated into his shell and spoke no more. We had time for little other than a quick cup of tea before the ticket office rang to say the London train was now leaving Preston.

The train came slowly to a halt and the four of us moved rapidly up and down the platform seeking an empty carriage. The train was absolutely packed! How could we watch Elvis in a crowded corridor with no cuffs?

'We'll luke in first-class compartments,' said Joe, showing some much-needed initiative.

We found one such compartment with just two other occupants. Elvis, Dave and I made ourselves quite comfortable. Joe slipped off the cuffs just as the guard's whistle blew and then gave us a cheery wave of farewell, from outside the slowly moving door.

Dave and I sat on either side of the compartment door; Elvis sat next to me. At the other end of the compartment sat two affluent-looking men in blue-striped suits and red-striped shirts. Elvis should have been wondering by now why I had not placed our non-existent handcuffs on his slim wrist. It was therefore time for a little bluff.

'Elvis, son, we have decided to treat you with a high degree of trust. We have further decided that we will not "cuff" you unless you give us reason to. We've both been specially selected for this escort. [Sergeant Cage would have liked that one.] I'm the British police half-mile champion, and Dave there is the Southern area middle-weight champion – and mean he is, too! Because we are going to treat you as a gentleman, we do not expect you to take liberties with us, understand?'

'Yer, a' course I do. Fanks, guv, you're a real toff!'

Dave, I thought, seemed just a little put out that Elvis did not appear to have included him in the accolade of being 'a real toff'. 'Put out' he may have been, worried he wasn't – within five minutes he was sound asleep! That's bloody marvellous, I thought, I daren't close my eyes now. I had visions of the train arriving in Euston with Dave and I looking like the babes in the wood and an empty seat beside us! If Elvis had legged it once to Manchester, who's to say he wouldn't do it again? Even assuming he had fallen for that running-and-boxing-championship bit, we weren't likely to be either quick or vicious if we were both sound asleep. On no account must I sleep!

Difficult though my problem may have been, it now proceeded to become twice as hard. A bump on my right side caused me to turn quickly towards Elvis. He had not only fallen asleep, but he was leaning on my shoulder! As I thrust him off, I noticed our two fellow passengers were also out like lights. I felt like the sole survivor of some Indian massacre. The next two and a half hours passed like an eternity, as I tried every trick I knew to stay awake. God only knows what facial expressions I adopted. My head tilted right, left, forward and back. I pulled in my chin – and I pushed it out. I opened my eyes as wide as I could – then I tried to open them just a fraction more. My eyebrows were lifted so high that my forehead creased like a prune (parts of it have never recovered). The train wheels assailed my ears with a persistent 'go-to-sleep, go-to-sleep' rhythm, and my brain could not understand why my eyes did not obey.

The four slumbering figures seemed to gain gradual life from the slowly breaking dawn. As we entered the north-west suburbs of London, the rain that had now fallen for thirty-six hours seemed to give up in exhaustion. A prairie of wet roofs stretched away in each direction for as far as the eye could see. That was in fact my last recollection, until I felt my shoulder being vigorously shaken. Opening my eyes in alarm, I saw Dave standing over me.

'Come on, we're here. It's just as well one of us stayed awake,' he said reprovingly.

Panic-stricken I looked for Elvis. He was standing up and combing his hair. I tried desperately to climb back into life. For a few seconds it was very difficult: colours and objects were swimming around and I could not assign them to any order. Three mail-bag-covered trolleys slipped by the compartment window. A distant hollow voice announced train times, from what sounded like a well secured dustbin. All four of my companions looked fairly well refreshed. I knew exactly what I looked like. I knew because I felt like absolute death!

'Stayed awake!' I echoed. 'Stayed awake! I've bloody well been awake all the way from sodding Wigan. I have been awake while all you sodding lot have been snoring your silly heads off. You in particular have slept like a bloody log. And as for him' – I pointed to the still combing Elvis – 'he's fallen all over me twice!'

'All I know,' said Dave, with a patience that he usually reserved for imbeciles, 'is what I saw when I happened to glance up. *You* were asleep.' He added that last sentence with an air of finality that had me boiling. If I had been less tired I would have gone for his throat.

'Excuse us,' said one of the pin-striped suits. 'May we squeeze past?'

The train had finally halted and our two companions were uttering their first words since we climbed aboard nearly three hours earlier.

Hundreds of people poured on to the platform; all around us other commuters were arriving on adjoining platforms. This was going to be a particularly vulnerable time. According to the yarn I had spun Elvis, I was supposed to be a sprinter. At that precise moment I couldn't have run to the toilet.

Taking no chances at all, Dave and I each seized a wrist and we marched our felon to the British Transport Police

Office. There we were made very welcome, with a cup of tea and some toast. I telephoned the station officer at Wharf Road Police Station and requested the attendance of the van.

'Where the hell have you been? You should have been back yesterday. You haven't lost the bloody prisoner, have you?'

''Course not, sergeant! What do you take us for?' I asked woundedly.

'I just thought perhaps you may have fallen asleep and lost him. It's happened before, you know.'

'We're not any old mugs, sergeant. We happen to be two very experienced coppers.

'All right, all right,' he said in a very relieved tone. 'The van'll be with you in about three-quarters of an hour.'

An hour and a half later found us three back at Wharf Road. Monday being quick changeover day, the early-turn shift was the same as the late-turn duty on Sunday. That meant I would almost certainly see Sergeant Cage. I had lots that I wished to say to that particular gentleman, but not before I had had some sleep – about four days of it!

'Well! Well! I do believe it's Chi-Chi the panda. What has happened to your eyes, 604, have they gone back into your head to look for your brains?'

I groaned at the all-too-familiar tone of Peter Cage.

'Listen, sergeant, in about fifteen minutes' time I am going to keel over and die. I will die from malnutrition and hypothermia. When I do, I would like the police force to know that it will owe my widow nine hours' overtime. Furthermore, I would like my family to know that I was heartlessly sent to my death by an uncaring sergeant.'

'Go on with you,' he answered. 'I bet you both enjoyed it really. You were bored to tears here yesterday. It made a nice change for you to travel on a train to Wigan. Incidentally, why didn't you take the station handcuffs?'

'We didn't need 'em, sergeant,' said Dave. 'We were warm enough.'

We handed the prisoner back to the station officer and Dave and I booked off duty. I automatically walked to the sidestreet where I usually parked my car. In my punch-drunk state, I could not think where I had left it. Elvis Presley Clements certainly hadn't nicked it, but then our manor had no shortage of the likes of little Elvis. Suddenly I remembered! I did not have my bloody car, it was in for repair!

My journey home takes twenty-five minutes by car; it takes two buses and one and a half hours by public transport. That is, provided the conductor would even let me on the bus. With my crumpled jacket, dark-circled staring eyes, two days' growth of beard and a tendency to keel over at regular intervals, I did not cut too impressive a figure.

Just before I reached home, I had to walk past my local garage on my way from the bus-stop. I decided to call in to see if my car was either ready or responding to treatment. Sitting on a spare wheel, just inside the door, was the local copper, who had called in for a smoke.

'Is that all you've got to do, mate?' I asked sarcastically.

'Oh, it's always so quiet on Mondays,' he answered, letting out a long thin stream of blue smoke. 'Sometimes I think Monday is the most boring day of the week.'

'Well,' I said, 'it would just serve you right if it was.'

The Bat-phone

One of the many innovations that have taken place in the force in recent years, is the personal radio. Today's recruits would no more think of setting foot outside the station without their radios than without their trousers (or skirts). But older officers have had great difficulty in coming to terms with them. Their incessant metallic chat restricts all forms of civilized conversation, and no radio yet issued is capable of being turned down at an acceptable volume. Their arrival coincided with the Batman and Robin series on children's television. Not surprisingly, the nickname has stuck throughout great areas of the force.

Even now, after some ten years of service, many of the early faults remain. They are cumbersome and difficult to carry, particularly in the summer when one has fewer pockets. They quickly wear out clothing, and the later models have nasty little aerials that explore nostrils and stick in ears. This aerial rises, phallus-like, from the left shoulder. To turn your head sharply to the right, will swing the back of the helmet round to such a degree that it can strike the aerial. When this happens, the helmet will swivel sideways and rest on your head like a pirate's hat. In short, I don't like them. The first day I was issued with one, it gave me such a headache that I tucked it up in my clothing locker and patrolled without it. Later in the day, on my return to the station, I was quietly approached by an old sergeant. He suggested I search my locker as quickly as possible.

'There's someone locked up inside it,' he said. 'They

have been chattering away all afternoon and perhaps now they would like a bit o' company.'

I took the hint.

Bat-phones are very akin to dogs. One can train a dog for a certain task and he will perform it beautifully – except when you particularly wish to impress. Then he usually looks at you as if you are some weirdo that he's never seen before. Bat-phones are like that. Ask them for the time of day and they work perfectly. With the right salesman, they could replace clocks. But try telling them you are fighting six armed lunatics on the roof of a thirty-storey building that is collapsing through fire, and all you get is a:

'Can you repeat? Your signals are breaking up.'

Sometimes, you may only receive a 'phut'. Imagine how you feel:

'They are pushing me over the edge! The floor is crumbling! The flames are leaping higher!'

'Phut!'

You can have no secrets with a bat-phone. When it splutters into life and a dalek-like voice demands: 'Give your location,' everyone at the station knows where you are.

'Oh! He was round there yesterday *and* the day before! What's he got there, then?'

Your mistakes are broadcast for all to hear. Every policeman since time began has made the most almighty ballsups; usually, no one knows except himself. As a recruit on the London streets, you are thrown into the deep end and there is just no way that everything you do will always be right. All you can hope is that nobody finds out. But with a bat-phone, everybody does find out – and immediately!

Two Wharf Road recruits decided to deal with a persistent milk thief at the nearby Co-op dairy. Early every morning, after the milk was delivered, several bottles were removed before the staff arrived. The thief lived nearby, in a turning close to the Co-op. While we knew *who* he was (Blackhands Michael!), it was difficult to catch him in the act, simply because his front door was only a few yards from the store of milk. The two recruits therefore decided to carry out an observation using their radios. On the first morning at 6.15 a.m. their dialogue began:

'866 receiving? 827, over.'

This sentence was repeated every few minutes until 6.30 a.m. Then silence until 6.40 a.m. Then:

'827 receiving? – 866, over.'

'866 from 827. I am receiving. Where have you been?'

'827 from 866. My bat-phone didn't work, so I went back to the nick and changed it.'

Silence until 6.55 a.m. Then:

'866, are you in position now? 827, over.'

'827 from 866. No, I'm at the nick again. My bat-phone didn't work.'

Silence until 7.15 a.m. Then:

'827 from 866. I am in position now. Are you?'

'866 from 827. Yes, I have the perfect hiding place. I'm behind this derelict car. No one can see me here. Where are you?'

'827 from 866. I am in Southland Square. No one can see me here, either.'

Silence until 7.45 a.m. Then:

'827 from 866. There is someone approaching. Can you see him?'

'866 from 827. No. My hiding place is so good I can't see out. Where is he now?'

'827 from 866. I don't know. I can't see him. Hold on! I have just seen him nick some milk. Let's get him!'

'866 from 827. What does he look like?'

'827 from 866. I don't know, I'm too far away to see. Can you catch him?'

'866 from 827. I can't get out, my foot is stuck. Where is he now?'

'827 from 866. I think he's gone into his house.'

'866 from 827. Do you know where he lives?'

'827 from 866. No, but almost everyone at the nick knows. We'll go back to the canteen and ask them.'

A few minutes later in the canteen:

'Er, does anyone know where the milk thief lives?'

At this point the observation was adjourned till 6 a.m. the second day:

'866 receiving? 827, over.'

Again repeated every few minutes until 6.30 a.m. Then silence until 6.40 a.m.

'827 receiving? 866, over.'

'866 from 827. I am receiving. Where have you been?'

'827 from 866. My bat-phone didn't work and I'm back at the nick changing it.'

Silence until 7.40 a.m. Then:

'827 from 866. Are you in position?'

'866 from 827. Yes.'

Again silence until 8.40 a.m. Then:

'866 from 827. Receiving, over?'

'827 from 866. Yes.'

'866 from 827. Some bloke has come along to this car where I am hiding. He's told me that the Co-op is not open today (Thursday) and therefore there is no milk outside.'

'827 from 866. Oh!'

'866 from 827. What shall we do?'

'827 from 866. I don't know.'

'827 from 866. Where does the bloke who told you the Co-op is shut come from?'

'866 from 827. Number 11, I think.'

'827 from 866. Let's go back to the nick.'

That little drama ended with the suspect virtually telling the two recruits that they couldn't nick him today for stealing milk because the dairy did not open on Thursdays! In the days before bat-phones, they could have slunk away, consoled each other over a pint and forgotten it by the following day. But now the story will haunt them for years!

Another problem with these wretched things is ninety-five per cent of the transmissions are for someone else. I find, therefore, I spend most of my time missing messages addressed to me and acknowledging messages for other people. This becomes doubly confusing when reception is bad. One hears just the odd word and is compelled to guess the remainder of the message, not always successfully.

A very nervous, yet at the same time dramatic voice, came over the air one dark evening:

'Splutter, splutter . . . the woman is petrified . . . phut, phut . . . it's the biggest one I've ever seen! . . . I need help! Splutter, RSPCA . . . splutter, phut . . . it's colossal! Must have assistance . . .' The transmission went dead for a while, then about ten people all came in together. Every unit which had received the dramatic message seemed to interpret it differently and saw the 'thing' in various forms. The snake interpreter was the first:

'Splutter, splutter . . . Hit it between the eyes and stun it . . . phut, phut . . .'

The flood gates were now open for anyone who'd ever fancied himself with animals; ranging from what to do with a giant Anaconda to an old gypsy remedy for a berserk hedgehog.

I settled for a fierce dog – no imagination, I suppose. I could see it all: 'frightened woman', 'biggest one he'd ever seen', 'send help!', 'RSPCA' – it all fitted. Yes, it had to be a dog. The next garbled message, however, placed seeds of doubt in my mind:

'Splutter, phut . . . it's just jumped fourteen feet up a tree!! . . . phut phut.'

The following transmission caused me even more misgivings:

'Phut . . . It's absolutely huge . . . nine inches across . . . and hairy!'

I'd had in my mind something after the style of an Irish Wolfhound, but what sort of dog is six feet tall and only nine inches across? It just could, I suppose, be the largest, narrowest and tallest dog in the world, but would a dog with a shape like that be capable of jumping fourteen feet up a tree? Somehow I doubted it. It was at this stage that my radio gave a weak little 'phut' and died completely. Bursting with curiosity, I made my way back to the station. I must find out what happened to the tree-jumping dog!

'Well,' said the embarrassed constable, 'it wasn't really a dog (or a snake, for that matter). It was a spider.'

'A SPIDER!!' I marvelled. 'That's even more impressive.'

'Well, you see, well, it's not quite as simple as that,' he said. 'When the message from the snake fancier was received about stunning it between the eyes, some brave soul, maintaining the highest traditions of the force, tried it.'

'Did it work?' I asked eagerly.

'Well, not exactly. He missed the point of aim on this six-legged elephant and in doing so he broke the thread – which had not been previously observed – which ran from the back of the spider. With a "plop" like a big jelly, a rather large (nine inches to be precise) PLASTIC spider struck the ground, leaving an innocent piece of black thread hanging ominously over the wall of the nearby fire station.'

Later, in the canteen, I forgot about my six-feet-by-nine-inches Irish Wolfhound; our snake charmer forgot his giant Anaconda; and one red-faced young copper did his best to forget the London Fire Brigade. It was unanimously decided that we would never have fallen for such an obvious leg-pull if it had not been for the terrible reception on those awful bat-phones.

The batteries that operate these radios are not without their problems. If one is attempting to understand a member of the public, for example, many policemen will remove the battery simply in order to converse. This is the sole means of switching the thing off. Of course one needs then to remember to replace it again. That nice quiet day that you have been congratulating yourself on experiencing, is often because the battery is in your pocket and not in your bat-phone.

Batteries must also be removed if there is a possibility of an explosion. When bat-phones were first issued we were unaware of this fact. Policemen would blithely tackle anything that may go 'bang' while chatting happily into their radios. Once suspicion was aroused, however, it was a very different matter. I mean, just think where they hang! A potentially explosive device, just six inches from my groin, tends to make me very nervous. Never more so than one quiet afternoon a couple of summers ago.

'604,' – me – 'Sturgeon Road junction with Danson Road, see informant – weird sewer cover emitting peculiar noises.'

What the hell is a weird sewer cover? I have my doubts about most calls addressed to me as a community copper. Usually I am given any assignment which involves family feuds, sick cats or little boys doing very disgusting things in a variety of disgusting ways. Really, I suppose, a 'weird' sewer cover could be a nice change. I was definitely curious as I cautiously slipped my battery from out of my radio.

I suddenly remembered seeing a science-fiction film in which a sixty-foot-high ant took refuge in the San Francisco sewerage system. (Why an ant which is sixty foot high should feel the need to take refuge anywhere was a little puzzling.) The ant gave off a peculiar odour and left mysterious deposits all over the place. This weighed heavily on my mind as I turned the corner of Sturgeon Road. I found myself looking for mysterious and foul-smelling deposits on the footway. Now if there was one thing that Sturgeon Road really had no shortage of, it was mysterious and foul-smelling deposits – none of which had originated from ants. Not deducing anything from the local aroma, I was obliged to use the more mundane approach, i.e., asking questions.

I addressed my first query to a skinny peroxide blonde who looked as if she was wearing someone else's teeth. Her answer was quite unexpected.

'Yerse, mate, blew it right up orf the bleedin' pavement, it did! Fahsands of sparks and filled the street with bleedin' smoke! I fort fer a moment old 'Itler was back!'

'Well, at least it wasn't an ant,' I said, half to myself.

'Bleedin' ants!' she yelled. 'Are you bleedin' mad?'

Before I could explain why it could have been an ant that was heaving sewer covers around, we were interrupted by an enormous crash. Opposite the scene of our drama was a tumbledown, derelict, Edwardian tenement. Above the windows, many of which were broken, was a heavy coping, almost a foot thick and about six feet long. Part of one of these copings had crashed to the pavement three floors below, leaving about two feet suspended from reinforcing wire, rather like a sword of Damocles.

'Oh! that's great!' said the blonde witch. 'Oh! that's bleedin' marvellous! The street's blown up and nah the bleedin' 'ouses are fallin' dahn!'

I toyed with the idea of asking her if she would stand underneath the coping, to warn passers-by of danger.

'Want any 'elp, mate?' boomed a voice. I turned to see a large and heavily tattooed man. 'I've got a gang working on demolition in the next street. What caused it?'

''E reckons it's bleedin' ants!' shrilled the witch.

I put on my official police constable's voice and explained that the explosion must have loosened the coping.

'Soon 'ave that dahn, mate,' claimed the good fairy cheerfully.

Sure enough, he was back in two minutes with a couple of fellows, both aged about sixty and slightly drunk.

'Nip up there, George, and whack off that coping, an' you, Arfur, sweep up the bits and pieces and put some trestles across the pavement.'

George soon appeared at a fourth-storey window, which he tried to open but failed. He promptly broke it and showered Arfur with broken glass. To my absolute horror, George, who was carrying an eight-foot pole, then climbed on to the crumbling ledge of a window, next to the one with the offending masonry. Casually leaning out into space, he wiggled his pole and tried to dislodge the remaining coping. Sixty feet below, Arfur was studiously engrossed in his task of sweeping up. He appeared impervious to the slivers of glass, small bits of window ledge and, to my mind, large bits of George, which were about to fall out of the sky.

After a few minutes, I realized that in spite of all of George's alcoholic acrobatics, the pole was some two feet short. George took slightly longer to sense this, but eventually yelled:

'Me pole's too short, Ted!'

Ted immediately showed by his receptive reply how the job of foreman had been rightly bestowed upon him: 'GITALONGERPOLE, GEORGE!'

George climbed back into the room, not without some difficulty, and almost immediately appeared with a longer pole. I had this fleeting, puzzling thought about the source of supply of those poles, but that vanished when I saw the size of the thing. It must have been twenty feet in length. George was now able to give the coping a right good wiggling and I ventured to suggest that now might be a good time to remove Arfur. Ted showed that he was big enough to take advice by calling Arfur to step back. I glanced at Arfur as he crossed the road to the sanctuary of the opposite pavement. I saw to my horror that it was filled with spectators, all hoping, no doubt, to be present when George fell to an 'orrible death from the window ledge. My horror increased when I noticed that the sewer cover was giving a volcanic-like hint that it was not the spent force I had thought it to be.

The pavement rumbled, sparks flew and smoke billowed from the surrounding pavement. The witch screamed: 'We're all gonna be bleedin' killed,' and the entire audience ran forward into the road, to escape the fires of eternal damnation that threatened to engulf it. At this precise moment, George's wiggling really paid off and the coping crashed to the pavement. George, spoilsport to the last, ruined the most dramatic effect by not accom panying it. Nevertheless, it was a most satisfying sight.

Anyone who has tried to keep a ghoulish crowd from any potential horror will know how difficult a task that can be, but the explosion worked like a charm. Within seconds the street was empty. Empty, that is, with the exception of George, Ted, Arfur and me. Arfur began to sweep up the mess as if nothing had happened.

Ted looked skywards and said, rather tiredly, I thought, 'Nah we've got ta git that twit dahn.'

George was endeavouring to climb back through the window but was having great difficulty because of the enormous length of the pole.

'I can't git it in the winder, Ted!' he yelled.

'FRO – IT – DOWN – INTA – THE – STREET – GEORGE!' called Ted, very slowly and deliberately.

George did and it only struck Arfur a glancing blow. Within the next half-hour, the three had managed to put some trestles around the danger, a road diversion sign had been erected and I was waiting for someone from the Borough Surveyors Office to inspect the damage.

A police car came slowly around the corner driven by the duty officer for that day, Inspector Winters.

'Is this yours?' he called, holding out a battery.

'I think so, guv,' I replied, feeling my empty pocket. 'Where'd you get it from?' I added.

'Some nutty blonde phoned the nick. She said she'd found it in the street and thought it might be the reason the sewer cover blew up. So she put it in a bucket of water till we arrived. Have you found out yet what caused the explosion?'

'Would you believe – ants?'

'No, not really,' he said, matter-of-factly. 'But on the other hand, I'd believe anything that happens round here. Don't lose that battery again, they're expensive.'

Twenty minutes later, another car arrived. An obvious borough surveyor alighted.

'Afternoon, officer. What has happened here?'

'Bleedin' ants, guv'nor. They've blown up the pavement, nearly killed Arfur, and the whole bleedin' street is in danger of collapse.'

'Oh,' he said.

I slipped the still wet battery into the radio and left the devastation in the excellent hands of the local authority. Life used to be so much more tranquil without these bloody radios. I gave a last look at the now quiet sewer cover. I do wish I could remember the name of that film, though.

Missing Persons

The first week in July had been hot and humid but now the weather appeared to be on the change. A south-westerly breeze had sprung up and an early evening drizzle slowly evolved into a steady midnight downpour. The rain slowly eased during the early hours and Monday's dawn was clear and sparkling. London looked set for a real summer's day.

Angela Deansley was a fifteen-year-old tomboy. She was a tall, lithe, attractive girl, whose slight facial birthmark served only to accentuate her ready smile. Her willingness to accept anyone, or anything, with the same cheerful humour, ensured her popularity both socially and at school.

Newington Girls, Comprehensive School was not the most sought-after seat of learning in the borough. Constant changes of staff plus an inability to attract the best teachers meant that pupils were always struggling academically. Angela took this situation in her stride. Though her sums may not have been good, her temperament was perfect.

It was two weeks till the end of term and most of the girls in Angela's form had already begun to specialize, mainly in the subjects that they expected to be taking for their GCEs the following year. Angela's three pet subjects, history, English and sociology, did not figure in the curriculum that afternoon. The many outside attractions that London could offer always seemed tempting, particularly on beautiful summer days. Angela and her constant companion, Penny Richards, had smuggled their swimming costumes into school that morning. They had thought about little during the early lessons except the cool waters of Kennington Park swimming pool.

The girls decided not to stay for school lunch and extravagantly spent far more money than they intended in the local fish shop, on chips and Coke. The resultant check on their finances revealed they possessed just 8p between them, nowhere near enough for a Kennington Park swim.

'I know! Let's go to the river,' suggested Angela. 'It'll be quite warm now – and it's free!'

Penny had misgivings: as a swimmer she was nowhere near Angela's class and in spite of the improvement in the pollution of the Thames, it still looked pretty grotty to her. Still, just to sit on the river wall and watch Angela's seal-like movements certainly seemed far more attractive than chemistry and biology in form 4N.

The tide was receding fast when both girls undressed beneath the steps that led down to the water's edge. Penny, after a toe-wetting paddle, decided she required no more exercise than a quiet sit on a rotting log. Angela, looking good in her brief black bikini, decided to swim around a couple of moored barges. Penny watched her with mild admiration, as she smoothly cut through the surface of the water and went quickly out of sight around the furthest barge.

'Harry!' called out Sergeant Miller, the late-turn station officer. 'Go round to 42 Peacock House. Their fifteen-year-old daughter has not yet arrived home from school. They're a bit worried.'

I glanced at my watch: it was just turned 7 p.m.

'Well, it's not that late. The girl has probably lingered with her school mates.'

'They say she's normally a good kid for time-keeping. Go round and show the flag, there's a good chap,' he added, somewhat condescendingly I felt.

I knocked at number 42 and almost instantly the door was opened by a lightly built, ashen-faced, middle-aged man. He led me straight into a comfortably furnished living room.

'Any news of her?' he asked anxiously.

'No, I was hoping you'd be able to help me,' I answered.

The other occupants of the room were a middle-aged woman and a rather pretty, open-faced young girl of about fifteen.

'This is my wife Rose, and this young girl is Penny – she is Angela's best friend.' He turned his head and I saw him wipe his eyes with his handkerchief. 'They went swimming today and on their way home – well, you tell the officer, Penny.'

I could see he was near to breaking up and I decided that now indeed would be a good time to switch conversation.

'Just tell me what happened the last time you saw Angela, luv,' I asked.

'Well, we'd been swimming in the river and on the way home she told me that she was a bit fed up and she was going to go for a long walk, just to have a quiet think, she said. I said she should phone home first, but she said she would ring later.'

'How later?'

'She didn't say.'

'Did she have any money or change of clothing with her?'

'No.'

'Any food, handbag or make-up?'

'No.'

I turned to Mr Deansley.

'Well, I wouldn't worry too much. I expect she'll be home fairly soon. They're a bit like that at times you know, young girls. They need a while to sort themselves out. It happens all the time. I'll make a few enquiries and I'll ring you before I go off duty at 10 p.m.'

Leaving Peacock House, I mounted my cycle and headed back to Wharf Road Police Station. I remember wishing that I had a fiver for every time I'd been called to a young girl with an emotional problem! I wrote out a missing person report and a copy was forwarded to Missing Persons Bureau at Scotland Yard.

Around 9.50 p.m. I telephoned Mr Deansley and was a little surprised to find that Angela was not yet home. At 10 p.m. I left the enquiry for the night-duty to follow up. I booked off-duty and called in at the Duke of Sutherland for a quick pint before I returned home.

Next day I reported for duty at noon and I was again surprised to find that Angela Deansley was still missing. Although the situation was becoming serious, we did have one piece of luck. A girl in the same form as Angela had reported seeing her that very morning. She said she had not realized that Angela was missing and the girls simply exchanged greetings and passed on.

'Where was this?' I asked.

'Wyndham Road,' she replied.

'Wyndham Road! Why that's barely 400 yards from where she lives! Was Angela alone?'

'Oh yes, quite alone.'

This was a very good sign. It probably meant that she wished to return home but was worried about what sort of reaction she would receive from her parents. I phoned Mr Deansley and told him the good news.

'Yes! I've also seen a couple of kids who've spoken to Angela. I told them to tell her that if she returns home we'll forget all about this little adventure. We just want her back – that's all. We just want our Angela back.'

For the next four days I did nothing else except pursue every piece of information to do with the case that came in the station, and there was plenty. Somewhere in the region of a dozen kids had chatted to Angela during this period and they all told more or less the same story.

A collation of all the conversations revealed that Angela was living somewhere local with a friend. Yet we had called on every friend she was known to have. She was in excellent health and spirits and she was roaming, quite freely it would seem, within ten minutes' walk of where she lived. Oddly, though, neither I nor her family ever quite managed to catch a sighting of her.

I then personally interviewed all of the children who had seen Angela. I spoke to them in their schools, in their homes and in the very streets where they had claimed to have seen her. Most of them I double-checked again, always hoping that something new would emerge. Yet still the same story was told. It just did not make sense; the girl had now been missing for five days. Fourteen youngsters had seen her and most had held a conversation with her. In spite of all these leads, we were no nearer finding Angela Deansley than on the very day that she went missing. The strangest part of the whole saga was not one adult had reported seeing her.

Together with six of my colleagues and several older and more reliable youngsters from a local youth club, we checked every single empty flat and motor car within half-a-mile radius of Peacock House. We discovered lots about local intrigues and love affairs, and even found a jackdaw-type pile of odd shoes obviously removed from the front of a local shoe store. But no sign of Angela Deansley.

Because of the many convincing sightings of Angela, the case was still classified as 'Missing Person' with no sinister implications, although I had long ago begun to have misgivings.

On the sixth day, I received a telephone call from the DI (detective inspector) at neighbouring Stone's End Police Station.

'Do you have a missing girl about five feet five inches, slim build and wearing a black bikini?'

'How old?'

'Difficult to say. Probably early teens.'

'Does she have a facial birthmark?'

'She may well have had – except that this kid no longer has a face!'

Apparently the body of a young girl had been found in the river wedged between the criss-cross pilings under a wharf. It would appear that she had been trapped for some days underneath a barge and each time the tide went out, the barge settled on her, crushing her beyond recognition.

I quickly explained the whole siuation to him.

'Okay,' he said. 'Let's get this girl Penny and her parents down here as soon as possible.'

Later that afternoon, the DI sat at his desk and Penny and her father sat just a little in front of it. I sat to one side, holding the Missing Person report in my hand.

'Now, Penny,' said the DI softly, 'can you tell me any more than you have already told the policeman?'

'No, sir.'

'Are you really sure? Think very hard.'

'No, sir – honest I can't.'

He then pulled open a drawer and removed a white plastic bag. He put his hand into the bag and removed from it a badly stained bikini, black in colour.

At that, Penny's lips began to quiver and she suddenly dropped her head on to the desk and sobbed uncontrollably for some minutes. It was all so predictable, predictable yet I hadn't got within a million miles of it.

When Angela had disappeared around the rear of those barges, Penny had panicked. The girls, after all, should have been at school. On impulse, she hid Angela's clothes and decided to say that her friend had left home for a while. The whole situation then escalated from there.

'But how about all those kids I spoke to?' I asked, uncertainly.

'Simple mass deception,' the DI answered. 'Very

difficult to see through, actually. Each of these kids was telling the truth, or at least their version of it. A schoolmate had received some sort of fame and they wished to be part of it. They just altered the day that they last saw her and presto! In their eyes they are now important witnesses. Happens all the time in murder investigations.'

'Well, coppers on bikes don't investigate many murders,' I replied a little churlishly.

'That's probably 'cause your cycle clips stop your circulation,' he said.

Angela's parents did not take to the inquest at all well. They could simply not accept that the body lying in the mortuary was Angela's. They fought the identification of the girl every inch of the way. Most of their savings was spent on employing a barrister. It seemed to them that as that unknown faceless child was not classified in law as Angela Deansley, then there was always the chance that the real Angela would one day walk in the front door.

I have never felt so sad in my life as I did on that Friday morning in Coroner's Court. To my complete astonishment, the Coroner brought in the verdict of accidental death to a person unknown. Even after all these years, Mrs Deansley has never ceased to give up hope, for in law Angela is still alive and well and about thirty-three years old. If that is so, then what poor child was under the barge?

The only person to have gained from poor Angela's disappearance was probably myself: I learned never again to make easy automatic assumptions when anyone is reported missing. It is difficult, of course, not to do this. At times there is almost a conveyor belt of mass-produced home-leavers waiting to be filed at our station.

As a general rule, few persons over seventeen years of age are accepted as missing persons. The reason for this is that if we accepted every wife or husband, sweetheart or lover who ever walked out on his or her partner, we would have time for nothing else. There are times when I feel that one half of the whole population of London must have just walked out on the other half. If a person has some mental history, or if they are very depressed, or if the disappearance is rather unusual, then they will be accepted, but it is very difficult to convince a spouse that the police cannot simply order the runaway back home. 'Now look here, Arthur lad! If you don't get orf 'ome to your Gladys a bit sharpish like, you're in dead trouble – I tell you!'

The strange thing is, there is no close season for runaways. On the face of it, it would be logical to assume that no one would be over-keen to flee in the winter, but it seems to make very little difference. In fact my two most persistent absconders seemed to disappear more during the cold weather than in summer.

Gracie Jarvis was a freckly faced thirteen-year-old kid who spent half of her time running away from an excellent home, from caring, loving parents. She was twice found during the bitter winter of 1963 literally frozen to the pavement. Frost-bite and malnutrition made little difference to Gracie's determination to hit the road. Just as fast as the police returned Gracie home, so she would run away again. She never offered an explanation, always claiming she didn't know why she went. The only reason why she never came to any physical harm – for she was a pretty child – was simply that it was just too bloody cold for anyone else to be about.

Likewise Rueben Mayers, who would also just 'up and away' with no reason. Rueben had always been a slight wanderer, but after being knocked down by a motor car he became much worse. He would simply walk out of the front door, just as if he were popping down to the local for a quick one. He never ever returned home of his own accord. He would usually be discovered by the local police thirty or forty miles away, in a state of complete exhaustion. Rueben was in his late sixties and, because his wife was an invalid, his son Peter would usually be asked to collect him. Peter Mayers must have collected his father from half the towns of the home counties.

Rueben did these walks for about ten years. Then, a year or two ago on the second of January, some road workers on a new by-pass in Surrey returned to the excavations they had left on Christmas Eve. One of their last tasks before the Christmas–New Year recess had been to lay a great lake of smooth concrete.

There, in the centre of this lake, at the end of a track of turbulent footprints, spread-eagled and face down, was Rueben. Cemented up to his knees, he looked like a crucified Christ-in-concrete. He had almost certainly died on Christmas morning through exposure and malnutrition.

Why do they go? Where are they heading? Each of them is missing, yet every one of them is different. The 'Missing Person Book' is a great leveller and it contains more human miseries and emotions than a decade of Sunday tabloids.

Some Drunks I Have Known

In a busy city police area such as Wharf Road, possibly as much as twenty per cent of police street time is taken up with drunks or drink-related problems. I have long felt that habitual drunks are not so much a police as a social problem. What can magistrates really do with an incorrigible drunkard? They cannot fine him because he rarely has any money to pay. Sending him to prison for seven days achieves little, for he will receive no treatment there and it just gives him something to celebrate on his release. Usually a small fine is imposed, say £1, with the option of one day's imprisonment. He will already have served that 'day', so he is therefore released to climb back on to the roundabout. Until drunks are regarded as a social problem police will always be society's dustmen, picking up the flotsam from gutters and park benches.

If a drunk pleads guilty before a court, then the presence of the arresting officer is rarely required. This was not always so. A few years ago, guilty or otherwise, the policeman had to be present. The inconvenience and wastage of manpower was enormous. On some nights it is impossible to walk down many busy streets and fail to see an arrestable drunk. This could obviously not be ignored by any passing police officer. So once you had arrested your drunk, come hell or high water you were required at court the following morning. Often, if your drunk was the first charge of the night, you could finish up being nominated for everyone else's. Or you could, perhaps, cut the cards, or even toss for it – loser takes them all! To finish night-duty at 6 a.m., and be back for late turn at 2 p.m. was bad enough, but to return again at 9.30 a.m. for court that same morning was evil. Sleep was out of the question. In some 'Not Guilty' pleas the drunk would be more coherent than the arresting officer (the prisoner was lying in a vertical position, your worship!). He was entitled to be; he'd been asleep all night. Policemen would therefore devise all sorts of ways to avoid arresting a drunk. This would not be without its complications.

I stood in a deep Walworth Road doorway at eleven o'clock one January night, with my number one priority obtaining shelter from the elements. In the distance, staggering down from the Elephant and Castle, I saw a short drunk in a long coat. He was all over the place, yet he was making some gradual progress in the direction of Camberwell. When he reached the traffic lights at the junction just in front of me he sought the black and white pole of the signals for support. He then began very slowly to slither down the pole in a spiralling movement. When almost at ground level, he made a supreme effort and regained an upright stance – but he didn't look good. I had an appointment the next morning with the police welfare officer: I was in desperate need of housing accommodation and he was my last hope. I had waited for some time for this interview and I had no wish to lose it. If I had to take this bloke to court I would be back to square one again. I just had to get rid of this drunk.

'Where're you heading for, mate?' I asked.

He swayed a little and appeared to point the top of his head towards me. This in turn made it difficult for him to see me. He then had to roll his head in order to find out where the voice was coming from. Once he had located me, he said, 'Manor House.'

'Manor House! Why, you're miles away and you're going in the wrong direction! You need an underground train from the Elephant and Castle. If you're quick you'll catch it. Go on, off you go.'

So saying, I turned him around and pointed him back from whence he came. He mumbled some protest but kept going.

My patrol that night included the rear of the shops in the Walworth Road. Having given them an hour of my attention, I returned to the main thoroughfare. I had thought I heard voices, but on closer study it was my drunken friend, returning once more towards Camberwell and talking to himself.

'You're going the wrong way, I tell you!' I said impatiently.

'Manor House, Manor House,' he repeated.

I looked at my watch. I was fairly certain that last train from the Elephant and Castle to Manor House had long since left. Still, he wouldn't know that, and there was always a chance that he might catch it. I again turned him around. He was now having great difficulty in keeping his balance. 'Manor House, Manor House,' he mumbled, as he toddled off towards the Elephant and Castle. I watched him move slowly, then resumed my patrol in the opposite direction.

An hour or so later, after my meal break, I returned to Walworth Road and there, lying on the cold pavement, totally incapable of any serious movement, was a little chap in a large coat! I groaned with self-pity. There was nothing else for it. I had to arrest him. One couldn't step over drunks lying on the pavement, not even in Walworth Road.

'C'mon, then, you're nicked,' I said angrily, pulling him up to some sort of a standing position.

He opened his heavy, tired eyes and, on seeing me, promptly burst into tears. His sobs were interspersed with the words 'Manor House, Manor House'.

Thirty minutes or so later, he was bedded down in the

cells. I used the opportunity to snatch a quick cup of tea before returning to the chill streets. Old George Rearsden was finishing his sandwiches, sitting in the only comfortable chair our canteen had ever possessed.

'Who's that you've nicked, son?' he said with mild interest.

'A bloke called Gerry Hargreaves,' I answered gloomily.

'Oh! Old "Neville Chamberlain", eh! I didn't know he was still about.'

'What do you mean – Neville Chamberlain?' I queried.

'He's been called that since before the war. He looks like Neville Chamberlain, him what used to be Prime Minister,' explained George through huge munches of bread and jellied brawn.

'You know him, then?'

''Course I do. I thought everyone knew him. He lives in the Manor House just down the road. He's lived there for years,' replied George, wiping his lips with the back of his wrist.

'Manor House! But that's an underground station over North London, surely?' I said weakly.

'Manor House round here, son, is the old kip-house down the road. Didn't he tell you he lived there?'

'Only about a thousand times,' I groaned. 'Every time he nearly got home, I dragged him off in the opposite direction and told him to catch an underground train!'

'Oh, he's going to love you in the morning,' roared George, choking on a fat crust.

After that night, if a drunk ever told me he lived in Buckingham Palace, or St Paul's or 10 Downing Street, I always took him to the Manor House.

If there was one drunk I dealt with more than any other, it was an Irishman named Michael Carmodel. Every copper at Wharf Road and all surrounding stations knew Michael.

He was a tall man of slight build, with a hint of a stoop, and a cap. I stress the cap because except for the occasions when he set foot in the courts I never saw him without it. No matter how drunk or in what position he found himself, his cap never left his head. Apart from his cap, he was unique in two other fields: he smelt – oh, how he smelt! And he was indisputably the world's worst singer. He unfortunately knew only one song, 'The Wild Colonial Boy', and he didn't know much of that. The lines he did know he would repeat for hours on end.

My first experience with Michael lasted three hours. People with a keener sense of smell than mine never knew how I survived it. He staggered along Walworth Road late one night carrying a bottle (what else?). Tripping on the kerbside, he slowly began to sink to the ground. He actually covered another thirty yards before finally becoming horizontal. Each step took him nearer and nearer the pavement. I watched in fascination; I thought his legs were shrinking. The bottle he so desperately clutched impacted first; then Michael's face. When I picked him up he was in a sorry state, with several deep lacerations to his cheeks. I had always tried to avoid calling an ambulance for particularly dirty drunks and Michael was a particularly dirty drunk. But in this instance I had no choice and soon we were in St Giles's casualty.

The pretty little student nurse had obviously never seen anyone like Michael before, and it showed. Staff nurses, however, are made of sterner stuff and one was soon talking to him in the voice that other people reserve for simple-minded, four-year-old, deaf children.

'You're – very – dirty. Where've – you – been?'

No answer from Michael.

'Er – he fell down,' I explained.

'How – did – you – get – those – cuts?'

Again silence from Michael.

'He fell on a bottle,' I said.

'That – was – very – silly – wasn't – it?'

Silence.

I felt I had to say something, if only out of courtesy.

'It could have been worse, it missed his eyes.'

'You – might – have – blinded – yourself.'

It began to dawn on me that this was perhaps the silliest conversation I had ever held. Michael suddenly looked at the staff nurse, as if he was about to speak. We all prepared ourselves.

'I want a piss!' he demanded.

'I'll take him outside,' I offered.

'Go – with – the – policeman – then.'

I could well understand Michael wanting a piss; she was beginning to affect me the same way.

We returned some minutes later and two young nurses began to clean up his face with surgical spirit. Although he never flinched when the spirit touched his many abrasions, his eyes never once left the bottle. Soon the last of the twenty-three stitches were inserted and Michael's treatment was completed. What to do now? I couldn't leave him in casualty. I thought I would try to see if he could walk on his own.

'Come on, mate, it's all over now. Off you go.'

Michael struggled up but there was no way he was going to make the door – he was still too drunk. I telephoned for the van and a short time later we were both in the charge room at Wharf Road.

'Turn out your pockets,' said the station officer.

Michael couldn't, so I began to do it for him. As I removed each article from a pocket, I would call it out for the station officer to check.

'One comb; one razor; five pence silver; two pence copper; four dirty pictures; one bottle of surgical spirit – '

Surgical spirit! I examined the label – 'St Giles'. Oh you wicked old sod, Michael! Fancy stealing from a hospital. Tut-tut, said the station officer. Michael said nothing. He was relieved not to go on the sheet for theft, he was quite happy to be just drunk.

I arrived home a little after 6 a.m. that morning and, because I was due at court with Michael, decided it was not worth going to bed. Around 7 a.m. I took a cup of tea up to my wife Joan who is a very heavy sleeper. Usually she requires two or three shakes to wake up. That morning when I entered the room her face was towards the door. I put down the cup and saucer on the bedside locker and moved forward to shake her. Her nose suddenly twitched like a rabbit. There were just two quick flutters, then her eyes opened wide in horror.

'Is that smell you!!?'

'Well it's Michael as well,' I answered woundedly.

Like most drunks, Michael led a charmed life. Having received a call at the station one Saturday afternoon, my friend Bert Ransom and I drove the van down to deal with 'six drunk men causing a disturbance'. On our arrival they all made off except one, who remained motionless on the pavement.

'Oh God, it's Michael,' said Bert.

I knelt down beside him and tried to get some movement going, making sure he wasn't injured or dead. He wasn't, just drunk. This time Michael would not only have to be nicked but carried as well. Neither of us relished that little task.

'Isn't there a stretcher in the van?' asked Bert.

The padded seats that ran parallel in those old vehicles lifted up and beneath them accumulated all sorts of treasures. I returned to the van and, sure enough, found a rusty-looking pair of hinged poles with green canvas sheeting folded between. The stretcher obviously had not been opened for years but Bert, a powerful lad, eventually forced the poles apart. We rolled the dead-weight Michael over on to it, congratulating ourselves on our good find.

Sliding the stretcher into the back of the van, like a coffin in a hearse, I closed both rear doors. Bert and I then climbed into the front seats for our journey back to the station. As Bert waited for a suitable gap in the passing traffic, the aroma arising from the recumbent Michael was first noticeable, then subsequently offensive.

'Phew!' puffed Bert. 'Can't we re-open the back doors?'

'Can't see why not,' I answered, looking down at the stretcher. 'After all, he won't be going anywhere for a while.'

I jumped down and ran to the rear of the van. Unlocking both doors, I hooked them firmly into the 'open' position. The strong through-draught provided an immediate relief to our suffering nostrils. Just in case the wind changed direction, Bert began to nose the vehicle impatiently out into the passing traffic. A flash of lights from a number 35 bus told him that it was clear for us to pull out and, waving an acknowledgement to the driver, we accelerated speedily away. The bus then tucked in comfortably behind us.

I stared almost unseeingly at the familiar road ahead. Suddenly I was vaguely aware of a movement to my rear. I turned casually, just in time to see the stretcher beginning to trundle its own way towards the open rear doors. These doors in turn led directly to the front wheels of a now fast-moving number 35 omnibus. We had both failed to notice that the stretcher was on castors!

'BERT! STOP!' I screamed.

The sleeping Michael's head, shoulders and cap were now out into the space between our rear doors and the bus's radiator. The stretcher then began to tip – and Michael began to slide! It looked like a burial at sea!

Everything then happened at once. Bert braked violently; the driver of the bus only now seeing the imminent danger, braked equally hard. I just managed to hold the wavering shafts with the middle finger of my left hand and the stretcher bumped back into position on the floor of the van. Bert and I looked at each other and raised our eyes in silent thanks. Michael simply slept.

The morning line-up of drunks at any busy London court is like a parade of the dead, or a chorus line of zombies. Most of them will have been arrested overnight and had some chance to sleep it off. Others would have well recovered from the original binge but would be experiencing withdrawal symptoms. Basically, they need a drink. The drunks are always the first cases to appear before the magistrates. The reason for this is that they can form as much as half of the entire morning's charges. If the court staff can get rid of them quickly, the place not only looks tidier – but smells sweeter!

There are, of course, occasions when a police station, too, can be snowed under by drunks. If a fight between a group of methers erupts in a local park, for example, it immediately places a great strain on our cell-space. Only in very exceptional circumstances, however, will two people be placed in a cell together. Occasionally, of course, it cannot be avoided. Then close supervision is essential. One particularly busy Saturday, when prisoners had been coming in thick and fast, two drunks were placed together in the first cell. On a routine check some few minutes later, the older man was discovered to be also coming in 'thick and fast'. He was instantly removed from the cell and further charged with indecent assault (his partner was asleep). On being fined £20 at court next morning, he claimed the entire exercise had been cheap at the price. He said he was so pleased that he was going away to save up another £20. I think he considered the opportunity to commit the indecency to be nothing less than an improvement in the station's amenities.

These 'amenities', both real and imaginary, are, of

course, an incentive for many drunks to be arrested. The cells may be barren and uncomfortable – but they are always warm. The food may not be marvellous – but it's regular and it's free. If a drunk is arrested after a court has sat on a Saturday, then he will not appear until Monday. He will, during that period, receive two full days' board, which will include at least six meals! It is by no means uncommon for drunks who have been refused arrest to smash a shop window adjacent to the station and wait calmly for police to arrive.

It is on cold winter nights that the attractions of the police station really begin to pull. A shop-owner telephoned Wharf Road in the early hours of Sunday morning to say that a man had been singing in her doorway for over three hours. The police van that was sent to deal with the call contained two good friends of mine, Bert and Harry. The van stopped outside the premises to the strains of 'The Wild Colonial Boy', sung horrifically off-key – Michael Carmodel had decided it was time to come in from the cold! Immediately the van came to a halt, Michael stopped his serenade and began to stagger from the doorway, reaching out for help to climb into the van.

'Who's going to court with him on Monday?' asked Bert, who always liked to know exactly where he stood.

'You can,' offered Harry generously.

'We'll toss for it then,' said Bert. 'That's fair, ain't it?'

'It would be – except that if I lose I'm still not taking him,' came the reply.

An impasse. Meanwhile Michael was showing some impatience and the opening words of 'The Wild Colonial Boy' could once again be heard filtering up to the shopkeeper's bedroom.

'How about if we dump him on Kennington's manor?' suggested Bert. 'They more than likely dumped him on ours in the first place,' he added, sounding hurt.

'You can dump him where you like. I've had him at court three times already this night-duty and I'm not taking him again. The magistrate will start to think I'm picking on him.'

'Anyone who sings like he does deserves to get picked on,' replied Bert ruefully.

Opening the rear doors of the van, they helped Michael climb aboard. Michael showed his gratitude by immediately ceasing to sing.

'Thank Christ for that!' said Bert, who had something of a musical ear.

Michael made himself instantly at home, lying down on the long seat and closing his eyes.

The vehicle had negotiated several sidestreets when Bert said, 'I think there's a car following us!'

Harry looked back from the van and saw it was a 2.4 Jaguar, in use at that time as a night-duty 'Q' car (plain clothes).

'It's only the "Q" car,' he said reassuringly. 'It's been a fairly quiet night, so they're probably wondering what we've got going on. Probably hoping there'd be some action!' He looked at the prostrate figure of the sleeping Michael and added, almost to himself, 'Bit removed from action, I'd 'ave thought.'

The van slowed to a halt in a quiet Kennington sidestreet.

'C'mon then, Michael! It's time to wake up,' called Bert.

Thinking he was in the nick, Michael wearily but quite cheerfully stepped down from the van. Suddenly realizing he was in foreign territory, he looked questioningly at the two coppers, as if suspecting a trap.

'Just hold on to that lamp-post for a minute,' said Bert.

Michael obliged and the van roared away. One minute later, the 'Q' car arrived and Michael was seen to be invited in. A charitable gesture indeed. Bert reversed the van into its bay in the Wharf Road yard and both he and Harry returned to the canteen to finish their meal-break.

'Van driver!' called the station officer.

'Sergeant!' answered Bert from the canteen.

'124 Camberwell Road – there's a disturbance.'

'I'll come,' said Harry.

Both officers climbed aboard the front seats of the van and it roared out into the deserted Walworth Road. The thud as Bert negotiated a sharp right turn caused both men to look behind them. Lying on the floor of the vehicle, having just rolled off the seat, was a very puzzled Michael Carmodel.

It was around this time that large areas of Southwark began to be vacated, to make space for the vast new housing estates of the 1960s. These clearances resulted in hundreds of tumbledown little houses being left vacant and derelict. Those few months were utopia for film-makers and drunks.

There always seemed to be a camera crew somewhere in the borough, usually making films about the wartime blitz. These films were all much alike. Mum wore a pinafore the whole time, the daughter was wayward and probably pregnant, the son died bravely in action, and Dad kept pigeons in the backyard. In the final scene of all these films, a bomb would destroy the house. The lovable little family cat and Dad's pigeons would miraculously survive. It did not matter how many films were made in the borough, the statutory requirement seemed to be: blow up the house. This scene was always great fun for onlookers. Arc lights would burn all night; actors would be half buried in bricks; and small boys would make small fortunes running errands to the local fish and chip shop. These shops would continue to serve until well past their normal closing time. The boys would pocket half the change and also scrounge a tip. The bystanders and spectators would enjoy the whole show, so everyone appeared happy. Well perhaps not quite everyone.

To slip under a pile of old coats, in a drunken stupor, in a derelict house, in a quiet street, in 1962, and to be suddenly awakened by air-raid sirens, searchlights, crashing guns, exploding bombs, blood-stained victims and little boys selling fish and chips in 1940, could be quite unnerving. Poor Michael found it so. Gathering his three coats, two bottles and one hat together, he fled from the crumbling ruins of 33 Abbotts Close. He amazingly staggered the half-mile to the Wharf Road enquiry desk where he was almost immediately arrested for 'creating a disturbance in a police station'.

'He practically fell in here, brandishing two bottles saying the Germans had landed, then he promptly pissed on the counter!' said Sergeant Rawlings indignantly.

Well, at least it was a novelty: it was about the one offence that Michael had never been arrested for.

The attraction of these houses almost proved the undoing of Michael. One night, in company with two of his friends, Michael sought the sanctuary of a first-floor flat. Feeling cold, they decided to build a fire. Although the fireplace was one of the few parts of the structure that still functioned correctly, they built the fire in the centre of the wooden floor. They then sat around it until they fell asleep!

It is extremely difficult to negotiate a path through these houses. Floorboards are missing, staircases are broken, rubbish lies all around, and, in this instance, smoke filled every room. The amazing aspect of the whole situation was that when my two young colleagues dragged the sleeping, steaming Michael from the brink of flames, he struck one of them on the helmet with a bottle. (An empty bottle of course, Michael was never *that* drunk.) The constable did not take too kindly to this and gave some serious thought to putting Michael back where he had found him. Humanity prevailed, however, and a '£5 or one day' drunk-and-disorderly fine at court next morning enabled Michael to resume his camp-fire life the following night.

I never saw Michael again after that day. He simply disappeared. Vagrants and drunks are always moving flotsam. Sometimes they stay, sometimes they go. Where they go, or why they go there, I have never been able to discover. There had been several fires in the old houses and two or three vagrants had been burnt beyond recognition. There was absolutely no proof that any of these were Michael, or any of the scores of other down-and-outs who probably disappeared at the same time. There is no one to report a vagrant missing. He leaves little behind him. No friends, no family, just a fond memory – and a terrible lingering smell.

Tight-rope

'Merry Christmas, Harry.'

'Merry Christmas, sergeant.'

'There was a phone query a little earlier that you may be able to help with. A lady telephoned from Liverpool to say that she is trying to trace her mother who she hasn't seen for thirty-two years and who used to live locally. She asked to speak to the longest serving copper at the nick. I've taken her number. As it's Christmas, perhaps you'd give her a ring?'

'Okay, sarge.'

Since it was a strangely quiet Christmas morning, I soon had an opportunity to telephone the lady. Dawn Pettigrew lived in a suburb of Liverpool with her husband, Tom. She had an intriguing and sad tale to tell. A tale so involved that it ultimately affected not only myself but my whole family.

According to Dawn, her birth certificate showed she was born Dawn Cecilla Wood. She lived with her parents, Sophie and George at 4 Binton Road from the time of her birth until she was farmed out to an orphanage some two years later. Dawn told me that she had spent all of her savings hiring enquiry agents, in an effort to trace her mother. While between them the agents had unearthed a great deal of information, they were unable to do the prime task for which they were employed, namely find Dawn's mum. The finances of herself and her husband having now run out, in desperation she wondered if perhaps a local copper from the old area, might be able to help. I said that I would do all I could and I requested as many details as she could give me. I further pointed out that this was not a normal task for a community copper to attempt. However, the situation did intrigue me and I would be happy to make such enquiries as may be needed, in my own time.

She told me that the enquiry agents had discovered her parents had been incompatible since long before she was born. George, having been badly blown up during the war, was in fading health. Sophie, on the other hand, was a lively, vivacious young girl, who had no desire to keep her wagon hitched to a rapidly failing husband. As a result, she had begun a relationship with a Canadian army sergeant. It had been an obsessive and passionate affair, which she had made no attempt to conceal from George. The sergeant had made all the usual soldier's promises but six months after his troopship steamed out of Plymouth Sound, the 7lb 9oz Dawn was born.

With the arrival of the baby, relations between the Woods became even more turbulent. As George's health faded, so Sophie's tempers increased. The final row resulted in the kitchen knife being buried up to its hilt in George's heart. 'Guilty, but the balance of her mind was disturbed', said the jury. Sophie Maude Wood was then remanded to a prison for the criminally insane.

What to do with the little Dawn then became a problem. She had been placed 'in care' for the duration of the trial but now something more permanent was needed. The father had been a non-practising Catholic while the mother was a non-practising atheist. On balance, the papacy won. A small Essex convent then took in the bewildered child. Dawn was to remain there until she was adopted a few years later. Her parents were probably well meaning, but the child soon began to rebel against the stern family discipline. This atmosphere became worse until, at the age of fifteen, the child left home without any idea where she was going, or what she was going to do.

Dawn was strangely a little hazy about the next period of her life. She said she worked in an assortment of shops but could not really remember in what capacity. In her late teens, she met and married a draughtsman some few years older than herself. She claimed she was superbly happy in this marriage and she had three children in quick succession. A few months after the birth of the third child, her husband decided to take the whole family to a remote cottage in Scotland for two weeks' holiday. The two adults plus the children and their luggage made the small ancient family car somewhat difficult to control over many of the mountain roads. Turning a right-hand bend, on a sharply descending road, they came face to face with the local milk lorry. The sudden swerve was too much for the old car's steering and it ploughed through a fence. A few moments later, it lay upside down in a mountain stream, about fifty yards from the road.

Dawn said the death of her husband and three children did not much bother her for the next three months. For the first month she was unconscious; and for the following eight weeks she was in a state of amnesia-shock. Slowly, after protracted surgery, she made a complete physical recovery. The deep scars on her head, however, were nowhere near as deep as the scars on her mind. She began to exist on a diet of sleeping pills and Valium.

Returning to London, she drifted around the Notting Hill area, sleeping in an assortment of squats with an assortment of people. She said she needed love to fill the vacuum left by her family. 'I would take love from anyone. Just as long as they showed me some tenderness. I would go anywhere and do anything.'

It was around this time that Tom appeared on the scene. They decided they were ideal for each other, and when he obtained a job in Liverpool the couple settled just outside the city, in Aintree. His work occasionally took him away from home. Dawn was still incapable of work and had little to do in their small flat, except brood over her life of misfortune.

'Once I had thought of tracing my mum, I found that I couldn't think about anything else. I just had to know if she was still alive. I didn't care what it cost me, I had to find out.'

I felt quite wrung out by Dawn's story and I began to make some local enquiries. While I could not find anyone who remembered the Woods – the street had long been demolished – I did find some help in the local library. In the voters' register for the years 1944 to 1947, both Sophie and George were shown as residing at 4 Binton Road. This in itself was unusual, since I knew that the old building, once a vicarage, had been requisitioned by the council in 1945 and was now a hostel. Further enquiries revealed that both adults were at that time employed by the council and 'lived in'. I traced the Catholic orphanage and spoke to one of the sisters who helped with several other leads. As a result I was able to give Dawn much more information than she had received from her private detectives.

Two weeks after receiving this information, Dawn telephoned me at the police station in a frenzy of excitement.

'I've found her! She's in Sheffield. She's sixty years old and she's very well. I've sent her some pictures of me, and Tom and I are going over to see her on Sunday!'

Dawn also telephoned the local newspaper, who agreed to drive her to Sheffield in exchange for the story.

That Sunday was my leave day, and on several occasions my wife and I wondered how the reunion was progressing. At eleven o'clock that evening, unable to wait any longer, I telephoned Dawn.

'It was absolutely dreadful,' she cried. 'We argued!'

'You what!!?' I exclaimed, incredulous.

'We almost fought, she was just so dreadful. She said I

didn't look like my picture at all. She said I looked like a cheap tart.'

Looking back, that incident should have sounded the warning bells – but it didn't. I implored her to give her mother another chance. After all, she had been quite mentally sick for a very long period of her life. Meeting her daughter after thirty-two years must have been an enormous shock. Surely the old girl was worth one more attempt? Dawn agreed and said she would call on her mother once again. The local newspaper had surprisingly decided against printing the story and were totally uninterested in any replay. This time Dawn and Tom were strictly on their own.

Their second attempt proved to be no more successful than their first. They wrote to Sophie, explaining their train arrival and departure. For good measure they even telephoned a neighbour who then relayed to Sophie their complete day's timetable. They also sent a spray of flowers by Interflora, which was to precede the couple's arrival by a couple of hours. Their presence at Sophie's door was greeted by total silence, explained by the note that read: 'Dawn, gone shopping for the day. Mum.'

It was becoming increasingly apparent that Dawn's determination to see her mum was more than adequately matched by Mum's determination not to see Dawn.

'That's it!' she told me on the telephone. 'The wicked ungrateful old cow. She can die now, for all I care.'

In an effort to prove that they did not hold me entirely responsible, Dawn and Tom invited me to Liverpool. I declined.

'Well, we are coming to London next week for a shopping visit and we'd like to take you to lunch as a "thank-you". It's for all you have done for us,' said Dawn.

By this time, I sensed that something was wrong, but I just could not put my finger on exactly what it could be. I made excuses for several weeks and each time they postponed their shopping visit. After two months' delaying, I finally conceded defeat and arranged to meet them at Euston, at midday the following Tuesday.

As I drove towards Euston station that sunny morning, I suddenly realized that although I felt I had known this couple for years, I had never actually seen them! My worries about identification proved groundless. About five hundred people alighted from that train and I recognized the pair of them instantly. They were exactly as I knew they would be. I saw Tom first. He was aged about fifty, with the same wide, striped, brown suit that I had pictured he would wear. Even his thinning, combed-back hair fitted my image of him. He wore a cream shirt and a gaudy green tie, the knot of which had slipped and was now about three inches long and half an inch wide. Everything he wore looked a size and a half too large for him.

If Tom was how I had imagined him to be, then Dawn made me feel an absolute prophet. She was of average height, stocky, almost aggressively built. Her complexion was pock-marked and she was heavily made up. Her eyebrows were wide rather than thick, and her hair, drawn back from her wide forehead by an Alice band, was not really long enough for such a style. The wide belt around her tight polka-dot dress bit deeply into her belly, as did her bra straps into her shoulder. Dawn Pettigrew was a powerful woman with something about her that was truly intimidating.

'Hello, Harry,' said Tom, striding eagerly towards me. 'How are you, Harry?' (How did he recognize me? Was I as obvious to him as he was to me?) Tom Pettigrew used my christian name, on average, about every sentence he uttered. 'This is Dawn, Harry. She's been looking forward to seeing you, Harry.'

Turning my attention from Tom, I was just aware of this powerful figure as it thudded into me. A meaty pair of arms locked around me and a large wet mouth washed my face. Her perfume had the delicate fragrance of carbolic and instantly made me cough.

'Hullow, dah-ling!' said Dawn breathlessly. 'I was determined to give you that great big kiss the instant I saw you. You're just as Tommy and I imagined you to be.'

'You didn't mind that kiss, I bet – eh, Harry?' laughed Tom.

'Oh-er, no, no-er, it was very nice, thank you very much,' I stammered.

'Well, we've lots to talk about, haven't we, dah-ling,' said Dawn fervently.

'What have you got planned for us, Harry?' asked Tom.

'Well, I thought we'd have lunch, then go to the police sports ground for a drink, then home to my place for tea, returning you to Euston in time for your early evening train.'

'That's really fine, Harry, that's really fine.'

I suddenly saw an age-long day stretching in front of me.

The next seven hours were, I think, the longest of my life. Tom was possibly the world's greatest bore. He would also try to anticipate every one of Dawn's fickle whims, and he always, but *always*, guessed them wrong. For her part, Dawn could make a sentence like: 'Oh, that's all right, Tommy luv, don't worry about it,' sound like a ruling from the Spanish Inquisition.

The only time I ceased to study my watch was during the hour when Dawn recounted the car accident that had destroyed her family. It was amazing how she had managed to amass so much detail. Her conversation on that topic was so lucid that I felt quite guilty about my reactions to the rest of the day. When she had finished her tale, I felt quite moved. She then delved into her spacious handbag and pulled out a small onyx statuette, about five inches in height.

'We bought this for you,' she said, surprisingly softly, 'just as a thank-you for all you've done.'

She did not hand it to me directly but walked over to a trophy shelf in the corner of my living room. Here she re-arranged some of my old sporting plaques, placing her award in the centre of the front row.

Some hours later, having dropped the pair of them at Euston, I thought that in retrospect my attitude towards them had been quite churlish. Any woman who lives through the trauma of having her family destroyed should at the very least be shown tolerance. In spite of my remorse, I also knew there was just no way I would ever see either of them again. The chemistry was somehow not right. I had served my purpose to the Pettigrews. I could be of no further assistance to them. It was a perfect time to take my leave.

One thing that had emerged throughout our telephone conversations was the inability of Dawn to live in harmony with her neighbours. There always seemed to be friction of some sort or other. Often her phone would be on 'interception' because she had received threatening phone calls. During her version of these arguments, I was quite surprised how many times her local police figured in the story. The other surprise was that every time Dawn recounted a story concerning local police, there were always two officers involved. Many of these calls were of a trivial nature and barely needed the attention of one. My early instincts of unease about Dawn had never completely died away. I suddenly had a very ominous feeling indeed.

A call to the headquarters of Liverpool's police force soon gave me the telephone number of Dawn's local police station. Apprehensively I dialled them.

'Do we know a Dawn Pettigrew? If you work at this nick long enough, mate, you're lucky if you ever get to know anyone else! If you ring Inspector Charlesworth at this station tomorrow morning, he'll tell you all about dear Dawn. He's our "Dawn Pettigrew specialist"!'

My call to Charlesworth next morning confirmed all my worst fears.

On introducing myself, he echoed 'PC Harry Cole from the Metropolitan Police, eh? So you're the very-senior-police-officer-friend of Dawn Pettigrew's, eh? I've been dying to meet you. Every time we get called to that house – which is about twice daily – she threatens us with you. How the hell did you ever get involved with such a scatty bird as her? She is so violent, she is practically a psychopath.'

I gave him a brief résumé of my relationship with the couple.

He listened quietly, then he said: 'Well, sunshine, you've got trouble. There is absolutely no way you can escape that pair. They just don't let people go that easily. Every time you as a police officer deal with someone like her, you are walking a tight-rope. I hope for your sake that you are a bloody good acrobat, 'cos with them you'll need to be.'

'Tom Pettigrew's harmless enough, surely? He's a bloody great bore, but that's about all,' I said.

'Oh yes,' replied the inspector. 'He's just a bit soft in the head. Unfortunately, he'll follow her to the ends of the earth if need be. She's been responsible for some terrible assaults in the last few years and in every one of them he has backed her up. She has masses of form, with a file as long as your arm. Were you ever alone with her?'

'No. They did come to my house, but he was present the whole time.'

'Christ! That's even worse. Our blokes are under strict instructions never to enter her flat alone. She'll make all of the allegations and he'll substantiate them! I think the best thing I can do for you is to send you her file, then you can see for yourself exactly how she operates.'

Two or three days later, I spent two gloomy hours reading the adult life-story of Dawn Pettigrew; née Wood; alias La Verne; alias Rochelle; alias Bowden-Lynsey. There was no doubt that she was Sophie Wood's daughter. She must have come as close to following her mum into the walls of Broadmoor as it is possible to get. She had convictions for numerous crimes but her most consistent trait was quite eerie.

She would read the papers avidly, in order to discover the story of a female murder-victim. Once she had a case in her sights, she would discover all she possibly could about the background of the unfortunate victim. This would extend to include the name of the senior detective in charge of the investigations. Once these facts had been established, she would anonymously telephone the number of the murder HQ. She would then insist on speaking personally to the senior detective in charge, accepting no one of lesser rank.

Dawn would then claim she knew the victim very well. She would add that the dead girl had purchased an unusual brooch on the day before she met her death. This could be vital news to the murder investigation team. There would have been no mention of the jewellery from other witnesses. The only description for the detectives to work on could therefore only be given by Dawn herself. She would describe a piece of her own jewellery in minute detail and then attach that very piece to the dress she was currently wearing. Still anonymously, she would give the police her own name and address as the prime suspect. Sitting down, she would then wait for the inevitable knock. The first detective to arrive would not only see a woman who had been suggested to him as a murder suspect, but one who was wearing the victim's brooch. Dawn would then not only protest her innocence, but also become extremely violent.

Dawn seemed always to be two people. The first one

was always trying to beat the second in some competition. This was in keeping with her habit of making friends with people and then trying to destroy them. The only reason why Tom had lasted so long was that she did not see him as a friend but more as an accomplice.

As I wearily pushed away the file, I suddenly realized that it had omitted any mention of her accident. I checked it again. Absolutely no trace. I quickly telephoned Inspector Charlesworth: perhaps this accident was the cause of her split personality?

'What accident? Not that fantasy about her husband and three kids? Did she tell you that one? Boy, she must have really found you gullible. Dawn Wood, Pettigrew, La Verne, or whatever other name you care to mention, has never had any children, neither has she ever been married. Not to a draughtsman, nor to that bird-brain who lives with her at the moment. She is incapable of telling the truth and cannot separate fact from fantasy. If anything happens to anyone she knows and the story appeals to her, then she just incorporates it into her own life-story. It's as simple as that.'

'Well, can we at least add to the file that her mother killed her father, or a man who passed for her father?' I asked.

'Yes,' Charlesworth agreed, 'provided it can be substantiated.'

Dawn seemed slowly to fade from my life from that day. It was true there were occasional messages left for me at the station, but even these became rarer. One Saturday afternoon a few weeks later, I returned home from my fortnightly penance of watching Millwall play football. At either end of my street, I noticed a couple of police cars. I paid no attention to them. It was, after all, my leave day and it is only on TV and films that coppers are never off-duty.

On reaching home, my wife Joan said: 'Your police

station telephoned to say that they would like you to ring as soon as possible after you return home. It sounded quite important.'

The first reaction any policeman has in a situation like that is to wonder if he has taken the wrong day off – I've been known to do just that. As I had just seen my team lose at home for the second week running, I just wished they had telephoned *before* the match.

'Are you all right?' said the station officer in response to my query.

'All right? 'Course I'm all right. Why, shouldn't I be?'

'Actually no, you're supposed to be very dead. At some time between five and six this evening you were supposed to be stabbed several times. Are you sure you're not dead?'

'The reports of my death have been greatly exaggerated. Now can you please tell me what this is all about?'

'Just after 3 p.m. today, a woman giving a name and address in Braintree, Essex – which turned out to be false – telephoned Scotland Yard to say that you would be stabbed to death between 5 and 6 p.m. this evening. Scotland Yard forwarded the message to us and we telephoned your local police. We did not wish to alarm your wife so we didn't tell her the reason. I would suggest you get a couple of local coppers to assist you to search your area. You can also – '

'No, it's all right, sarge,' I interrupted. 'You can call off the hounds. I know what this is all about. You can leave it to me now.'

I telephoned the local police and asked them to call off the two police cars.

Soon I had forgotten all about Dawn's drama.

I was reminded of it next day, however, when there were three more threats to my life. This was now becoming rather silly. Fortunately, my wife Joan and my daughter Christine are level-headed people, so the whole thing was just a bore. One consolatory aspect for me was the thought of Tom's phone bill.

On the following Monday I had a long interview with my chief superintendent and, subsequently, another conversation with Inspector Charlesworth. The Liverpool police now had an extensive dossier on Dawn's activities. She was about to be arrested for several offences totally unconnected with me. I made a written statement concerning my experiences with the couple and waited to be called to Liverpool to give evidence. In the event I was not required: they both pleaded guilty to all charges.

I heard nothing more for a few weeks, then I heard that Tom had been given a period of probation and Dawn had been remanded for medical reports.

That was the last I ever heard of them. I could never bring myself to telephone, even to hear the court's final verdict. It is quite surprising to me just how the couple seem to have disappeared from my memory. Just occasionally, though, they slip back through the mist of time. Alongside my trophy-shelf rests my telephone. Sometimes when answering, the caller may take a few seconds to state his business. In those silent seconds, which can sometimes seem an age, I find myself instinctively glancing at the statuette. Somehow I have never been able to bring myself to discard it, perhaps because of the inscription. It simply reads: 'With thanks, Dawn and Tom'.

Football Hooligans

There had been nothing like it since the Mad Hatter's tea-party; all it lacked was Alice.

About 150 coppers of all shapes and sizes were scattered around the dining hall, attempting to come to grips with a small braised chop, two scoopfuls of mash and a scattering of fresh-frozen peas. Their insurmountable problem was that St Edward's School, Castle Street, London E6, adjacent to the West Ham Football Club, was in fact a primary school. It therefore contained only primary school furniture.

Table-tops sloped from their knees like the decks of sinking liners; weak brown gravy streamed from unbalanced plates; and large heavy bums smothered frail tiny chairs, many by as much as six inches.

'Your attention please, gentlemen!'

A smart young chief inspector strode purposefully into the hall to begin his briefing. He took just a few minutes.

'Because this is an all-ticket, quarter-final cup-tie, the south end of the ground has been allocated to the Aston Villa supporters. That is where you will be. It will be a capacity crowd, so there will be little opportunity for any groups to go rampaging around during the game, but there may well be some trouble before and after the match. When the final whistle blows, keep all of the Villa supporters exactly where they are – none is to leave. Then, when the West Ham crowd has finally left, we will escort all of the Villa fans to Upton Park underground station. Some of you will then accompany them on the train, at least as far as Barking railway station. Coaches will then be despatched from here to pick you up and return you to the stadium. Oh, one last thing,' he concluded. 'In the previous home match, we discovered one little hooligan wearing an eye patch. This was in fact a pretence. During the game he used it as a sling-shot. It fired nails.'

'I'll keep an eye out for him,' my companion Lou Peters called out. 'At Arsenal last week I saw a bloke with two eye patches and a white stick,' said another comedian. 'I reckon he must have been a master hooligan,' he added thoughtfully.

The usual banter at these pre-match briefings hid the appalling fact that in most professional matches played nowadays the opposing crowd has to be escorted back through enemy territory like renegade Indians being returned to their own reservation.

About an hour and a half before the kick-off we took up our positions on the terracing behind the south goal. The ground was virtually deserted. Coppers stood around in twos and threes, making small talk and repeating the jokes they had heard last week at Chelsea, Tottenham or Crystal Palace. Soon, up the steps at the rear of the shed, people began to emerge, trickling slowly out to all parts of the ground.

About an hour before the kick-off, the trickle became a flood and the Wharf Road contingent of police (about fifteen men and one girl) paired off and spread themselves across the terracing, along a central gangway.

The chanting and counter-chanting of the fans became louder and more venomous, particularly in the south-west corner of the ground. Here, each opposing set of supporters was separated by a fence, two policemen and a woman police constable who was in her first six months of service. It was fairly obvious that this place, being the only point of contact between the sets of rival supporters, would be the most likely location for any eruption.

As the kick-off time neared, many youngsters became more and more frenzied. The sheer hatred on the faces of some of these kids was quite terrifying. A great number of them were similarly dressed. They wore brown 'bovver' boots, tight jeans or cords, braces and a tee-shirt. The tee-shirts ranged in colour from off-white to pale black. Many of these shirts sported obscene slogans which most of the wearers appeared totally incapable of reading or writing. Their heads were closely cropped, with as little as half an inch of stubble remaining all over the head. Some of these hair-cuts had the West Ham badge – a pair of crossed hammers – shaved closely on to their skull. I studied the backs of these heads intently, to discover any scar that would indicate that the brain had also been removed, but no such sign was apparent.

By ten minutes to three, I had reached the stage where I was glancing nervously at my watch every few seconds. Ten minutes to kick-off and an awful lot of things can happen in a football crowd in ten minutes. This section of the crowd was boiling and it needed a distraction. It soon received it.

An arm came swiftly up from the most belligerent section of the West Ham crowd and a glass, three-quarters full of urine, sailed over scores of heads and miraculously never shed a drop – that is, until it hit the neck of the young WPC. The roar of delight that came from hundreds of throats piled on the agony for the poor girl. She had just learned a golden rule the hard way: never turn your back on a hostile crowd. It was impossible to see who threw the glass, but every PC in the vicinity mentally logged the area from whence it came.

An enormous roar from the part of the crowd opposite the players' tunnel, and a flurry of photographers, indicated that the teams were about to emerge on to the pitch. This would take a great deal of heat out of the situation. West Ham wore their well-known claret and blue colours, but Aston Villa, being the away side, were wearing unfamiliar white shirts.

The game itself was quite good. With less than a minute to go, there was no score, although either side could have taken the lead on several occasions. Just when the West Ham fans were resigning themselves to a mid-week away trip to Aston Villa – and the Villa fans were hoping that the ground advantage would get them into the semi-final – a white-shirted arm went up and touched the ball in the Aston Villa penalty area. Penalty!

The stunned silence from the Villa supporters that crowded, white-faced, around me seemed strangely to swamp the roar of delight from their West Ham counterparts just over the fence. The more nervous fans of both sides covered their eyes as the referee placed the ball on to the penalty spot. Stuart, the West Ham full-back, nervously adjusted the ball to his own satisfaction. He took a few paces back and, with a few quick strides, thumped the ball into the back of the net. Goal!

There was barely time for the game to be restarted before the referee whistled for time.

The vast majority of the West Ham fans shuffled happily away towards the exits, understandably delighted. Dads with their small sons perched on their shoulders chattered happily away, reminiscing of former glories. Workmates, drinking partners, neighbours and families – the same happy faces that could be seen on any ground all over the country when their team had won. The Villa fans, by contrast, stood in a huge muted group, barely able to talk. Some moved towards the exits shaking their heads in disbelief, only to be turned back by two coppers. 'Villa supporters? Sorry, you can't move off just yet.'

They said nothing, they nodded and turned silently back, like the bewildered inmates of some concentration camp.

The hard core of the remaining West Ham supporters showed no sign of leaving the ground and about two hundred of them began to assemble close to the fence that had separated the two sets of fans. Suddenly, one of them climbed the wall that ran round the perimeter of the pitch. He then ran diagonally across towards the Aston Villa fans. Immediately he was followed by a howling, screaming mob. The Villa supporters had no such organized 'hard core'. Their 'shock troops' were scattered in twos and threes all across the terracing. The first impact of the assault therefore took place against the soft underbelly of the Villa supporters – the dads with young kids, the middle-aged and the elderly. They reeled back from the pitch wall.

The loudspeakers crackled into life: 'Now come along, lads, do keep off the pitch.' I had never before heard anything that galvanized me so quickly into life as that innocuous and impotent 'Now come along, lads . . .' The same thought applied to each of my colleagues.

There is no doubt that the mob would have disregarded any appeal, no matter how eloquently delivered, but this futile sentence was less effective than Canute's chair. The entire section of policemen in that corner of the ground, some twenty in number, then climbed the pitch wall and met the charging horde around the touchline. For three or four minutes it looked like a mammoth brawl. Eventually the fans were pushed back, literally, over the wall. Foremost amongst the coppers in the action, was the huge, bearded, twenty-two-year-old Murdo Durrant. Murdo had been a frantic West Ham supporter all of his life and had cheered out loud when West Ham had scored!

Throughout this confrontation the crackling voice could be heard: 'Now please, lads . . .' 'Come along, you boys . . .'

I asked one sixteen-year-old youth that I grabbed why he and his kind seemed so intent on ruining the game that

I loved. His narrow, glazed eyes stared at me in genuine puzzlement.

'We gotta, ain't we? They're Villa, ain't they?'

That for him was a justifiable, honest reason for his behaviour. The fact that it wouldn't have mattered had the opposition been Arsenal or Accrington Stanley never entered his empty head.

A procession of policemen each led away a protesting youth. The remainder of us removed the flotsam from the pitch: a couple of darts, a few sharpened pennies, and numerous bottles and cans. We then turned to our next task, escorting the visiting fans to safety!

We formed them into several large groups and walked with them to nearby Upton Park station. Our instructions were to accompany them on to Barking, which is about two and a half miles away, two stops down the line. Other than verbal abuse, our march to the station was uneventful (the steady rain that now fell probably contributed to that).

On our approach to Upton Park station, a blurred voice announced over the tannoy system that the next eastbound train calling at Barking was already waiting to leave. Everyone broke into a run. Well, perhaps not quite everyone, because in all of the careful forward planning that had taken place, one important detail had been overlooked: hardly any Aston Villa supporters wished to go to Barking. In fact, they walked to an entirely different platform and caught a train going in the opposite direction – to central London!

We now had an interesting problem. Our coaches had left West Ham stadium and were heading east. Our charges were leaving Upton Park station and heading west. If we went west, God knows where we would finish up, or what time we would arrive there. The situation was further complicated by Murdo Durrant: it was his birthday, and a party was due to be held that evening. The thought of celebrating a twenty-second birthday on a crowded train full of morbid Aston Villa supporters and finally arriving in Birmingham had no great appeal for us. We therefore went east, to Barking.

Every Saturday afternoon and many weekday evenings throughout the football season, that situation, with all its expense and inconvenience, takes place. Kids who don't really know a football from a brass-spittoon would not dream of missing a game. They never watch the play, or the finer skills of the game. They just watch the other team's supporters. To be fair, not every crowd is that bad. Just occasionally one sees not just a game but a spectacle that is both enjoyable and memorable; not always, however, for the football.

'We hate Not-ting-ham Fo-o-o-r-est . . .'

The traditional pointless chant that can be heard at every football ground up and down the country every Saturday afternoon throughout the season reverberated around the packed Wembley Stadium. Perhaps not quite so 'pointless' on this occasion because Wolverhampton Wanderers' opponents this chilly overcast March Saturday were in fact the European Champions themselves, Nottingham Forest. The small contingent of Wharf Road constables, under the direction of newly promoted Sergeant Wilkins, were spread thinly out in the numerous standing enclosures at the end of the ground that had been allocated to the Wolverhampton supporters.

Prior to the kick-off, my own soccer loyalties had been equally divided. I certainly admired the achievements of Notts Forest but I felt that it would have been nice to see a different name engraved on the League Cup. If I had been undecided in my preference of winners before the game, being a solitary copper shut up in a small enclosure with a couple of thousand fans all talking like Jasper Carrott convinced me – for that afternoon at least – that I should prefer a Nottingham Forest victory. The enclosures at Wembley are very similar to cattle-pens, designed to make crowd control easier. It doesn't always work.

As a general rule, football fans rarely attend Wembley more than once throughout their lifetime. With only four clubs out of the eighty-eight in the football league being able to play there each season, usually only the elite arrives. The result is that a fan who has a ticket in his pocket feels he can have a leisurely drink in the centre of London and arrive at the stadium a few minutes before, or in many cases after, the kick-off, then watch the match in comfort. Nothing could be further from the truth.

If a supporter arrives any less than ten minutes before the kick-off, he could, with a great deal of luck and providing he stands on one foot, see as much as three-quarters of the game. If he arrives ten minutes after the kick-off, he'll see little more than a row of boils on the neck of the one-footed supporter in front of him. He would then be well advised to leave the maelstrom, return to the car park and listen to the game on the radio.

In an effort to combat this problem, the stadium authorities employ staff to pack in the early arrivals tightly at the front of the enclosures. The problem these packers face is the in-built resentment of the average football fan to be 'packed'. If a supporter arrives one and a half hours before the kick-off, he feels, understandably, that his early arrival at least entitles him to stand where he likes. Usually a policeman is on hand in case a fan becomes really obstructive. This task becomes progressively more difficult as the enclosures fill up. Eventually, no room is left for either packers or policemen. When the referee sets the game in motion, there are usually a couple of hundred people still edging their way up the steps that lead to each enclosure entrance. Meanwhile, of course, there is ample room at the front but no means of securing access.

In an attempt to assist this packing, I climbed on to a

six-inch concrete ledge at the rear of number 9 enclosure. Perched precariously above the crowd, I yelled out directions every few seconds:

'Go right!'

'Move down at the front!'

'Don't push, you silly bugger!'

The idea seemed to work, at least until the teams emerged on to the pitch, when I finally lost it. I then decided that it was a good time to relinquish my vantage point. Unfortunately, the crowd had become so packed underneath me that there was no room for me to descend. I spent the entire duration of the game six feet above the crowd, balanced on my heels, crouching under a girder and clinging on by the finger-tips on my left hand. I had a great view of the game but I was paralysed for a week.

Midway through the second half, the Wolves' centre-forward, Andy Gray, scored the only goal of the game. The fans in number 9 pen went delirious. Thousands of them linked arms and jumped up and down. The vibration across the concrete flooring was akin to an earthquake measuring ten on the Richter scale. Banners were waved, toilet rolls thrown, and drunks slipped quietly down into oblivion. I prayed that Forest would not equalize. I didn't relish spending thirty minutes of extra time screwed up on this wall.

Eventually, referee Richardson blew his whistle for time and the usual Wembley cup presentation took place. The players filed up the narrow wooden staircase and into the stand. There, in front of the royal box, they received their medals, and their captain held the cup aloft to the adoring crowd. The Wolverhampton team then returned to the pitch and began to make their triumphant circuit. It was at this moment that I first realized the opposite end of the ground was already empty! The disappointed Notts Forest supporters had simply melted away. The Wolves fans at my end, however, showed no such signs of wishing to leave. It was not until the last of the players had disappeared into the tunnel that the first of the Wolverhampton fans began their reluctant trickle. Thirty minutes later, those grey terraced steps were covered only by sheets of whirling newspapers, rolling empty beer cans and the great lakes of urine that only a football crowd seems capable of passing.

Up to a point, the task of the Wharf Road contingent was completed. For scores of other policemen – those outside the ground on traffic-points and car park exits, for example – it was only now beginning. We were therefore kept waiting as a reserve body outside the main gates until the last of the crowd had left the stadium and its precincts.

This was a good opportunity to explore the stadium itself. A biting north-east wind provided one good reason for seeking the shelter of the grandstand. The other and infinitely greater reason lay in the shape of a chief superintendent who carried a personal radio. Now if there is one thing I have learnt in my years in the police force, it is to beware of chief superintendents who carry personal radios. They are far more dangerous than the Ides of March or Greeks bearing gifts. I am never sure exactly what gets into them on such occasions but they remind me of elderly ladies who suddenly acquire Aston Martins. Their whole character undergoes dramatic changes. It doesn't matter how smooth or well-running a situation is, give a chief superintendent a personal radio and he will feel obliged to balls it up. (The situation, not the radio, although some have been known to do both.)

The potential of this bloke, plus a very young sergeant with a dozen constables with apparently nothing to do, struck me as being disastrous. Within a few minutes he would have us rushing about all over Wembley dealing with incidents large, small and imaginary. I suggested to Sergeant Wilkins that now might be a good moment to check on the security on the inside of the stadium. The young sergeant readily agreed and we filed through the huge stadium doors.

On the approaches to the pitch itself was a small mountain of flowers, mainly carnations. These had formed part of the floral arrangement in front of the stand and they were now being thrown into waste sacks. Woman Police Constable Ann Jones, a pretty young Devon girl, began to salvage the best of the blooms and passed them among the rest of her male colleagues, pinning a bloom into each whistle chain. Eventually even this palled and one by one we sat down wherever we could, our coat collars turned up and our gloved hands thrust deep into our pockets. It was now completely dark and the cutting wind seemed trapped in the bowl of the stadium. At times it seemed to pick us out individually, attacking our faces with a roaring blast. Although the gusts would fade as quickly as they began, the fragile scent of the carnations would linger strangely in that turbulent air.

I sat on the bottom of the wooden staircase that led up to the royal box. I had retreated into my overcoat like a frozen tortoise.

'Er – excuse me. Can we touch that step please?' said a nasal Black Country voice.

I looked up to see two crumpled figures, both sporting the 'Old Gold' rosettes of Wolverhampton Wanderers. I did not need any explanation of their presence, their eyes told it all. They had obviously become drunk and missed the game. Finding themselves marooned in an obscure corner of the locked stadium an hour after the end of the match, they were now desperately seeking a way out. However, as cold as they were, there was no way that they were going to pass up an opportunity to touch the steps that their heroes had climbed some sixty minutes earlier.

'You can do better than that,' I answered. 'Follow me.'

With that, I plucked the carnation from Annie Jones's

tunic and led both newcomers up the wooden staircase.

The three of us reached the top and turned left along the famous narrow walkway, filing past the royal seats. I stepped over the wall, reached back and shook the hand of each of my companions. I then handed them each a carnation and said:

'Wave to the crowd, then.'

As they turned to face the dark empty stadium, a roar of applause and cheering broke out from the twelve coppers below.

I looked anxiously about us, thinking that perhaps the joke had gone far enough, and gently shepherded both fans down the steps and back on to the pitch. Each had tears in his eyes. The older of the two was so emotional that he wrung my hand and said:

'My baby daughter is eighteen months old and she ain't ever goin' to forget this day. Thank you! Thank you! Thank you!'

I was completely taken aback by the intensity of their gratitude and rather uncomfortably led them out through the main gates and into the car park.

On my return to my colleagues, I plucked another carnation to replace the one that I had taken from Annie.

'Do you think he is going to tell his baby daughter that story for every day of her life?' asked Ann, as I handed her the flower.

'I'd love to be there when he tells his work-mates on Monday morning. I bet he'll get quite belligerent when they don't believe him,' I replied.

'All in the coach, lads. You're dismissed!'

We turned to see the inspector from the radio control van striding towards us.

Exactly two hours after the final whistle had blown, our chartered coach slowly rolled out of the Wembley car park. As I turned to look back at the great cold stadium, I could just make out the figure of the chief superintendent at the top of the main staircase. He appeared to be holding his radio against his ear.

'Like Nelson on the bleedin' bridge,' murmured a quiet voice from somewhere at the front of the coach.

'Well, someone better tell 'im the fleet's gone,' came the sleepy rejoinder.

A Very Good Trooping Indeed

Every police station in London carries among its library of documents 'the parade book'. This is a very large notebook that contains a whole mass of jumbled information which would be difficult to classify elsewhere in the station. It is so called because it is supposed to be read by each officer when he or she 'parades' at the beginning of each day's duty. It is in fact a discipline offence not to read the thing. In the parade book one will discover which local burglar alarm is broken, who is playing in goal for the station football team and if the National Front has ruined yet another of your Sundays off. Whenever a person sees their name entered in the book, they are required to acknowledge the entry by inserting the letter 'W' alongside. This action denotes they have been 'warned'.

An entry for that early June Tuesday caught my eye. Sandwiched between a complaint from a shopkeeper that someone persisted in urinating in his letter box and a letter of thanks from a voluptuous young lady, whom half the nick had apparently assisted when her car had broken down, was the following entry:

> The undermentioned officers will be aid to 'A' District for the Trooping the Colour ceremony on Saturday, 11 June 1977. Parade 7.45 a.m. at Wharf Road, for coach leaving at 8 a.m. This being the Silver Jubilee year, a particularly high standard of dress is expected.

Among the list of names and numbers was mine: PC 604M Cole.

The paragraph relating to a high standard of dress is arguable. The Metropolitan Police no longer has a ceremonial uniform. Every article of clothing worn on these grand occasions also has to be worn on everyday street duty. While the wearing of trousers and tunics can at least be rotated, nothing much can be accomplished with raincoats. They are in use most days even when, as quite possible, they have been soaked through the day before. That Jubilee summer had been exceedingly wet and most coppers' macs already looked like quilted car-covers, mine no exception. I just crossed my fingers and hoped for a nice day.

Some policemen develop a preference for the occasional duty away from their own station. Many, on the other hand, do not. While I probably belong in the second group, it would be fair to say that I always enjoy Trooping the Colour. This ceremony always takes place in June, with the two previous Saturdays set by for rehearsal. I always enjoy any pageantry that features the Household Cavalry. To spend three spring Saturday mornings in, or adjacent to, one of London's lovely parks never seems to me to be actually working for a living. Therefore, usually around mid-May, I seek out the duty sergeant. I then give him a gentle reminder that, like the Queen herself, PC 604M Cole is alive and well and available for the Trooping the Colour ceremony. He is not always impressed.

A great problem I have had throughout my whole police service has been my time-keeping. It is frankly abysmal. I never intend it to be so, it just works out that way. I begin most days by running down the garden path still eating my toast. Five minutes later I travel the same path again – having forgotten my car keys. That Saturday was no exception. Having twice returned home, first for my keys and second for my cash, I arrived at the station at 7.55 a.m. Slipping quickly into my uniform and still securing my buttons, I ran quickly into the parade room where twenty of my colleagues were already assembled.

Sergeant Peter Cage looked up from his clipboard: 'Ah, Cole! How nice of you to have found the time to join us! I fully realize that you have done this parade about as many times as Her Majesty but there are certain little boring formalities that the rest of us have to go through – such as reporting for duty on time. Do you think it would have suited you better, perhaps, if the Queen had given you a call just before she left the Palace? If it's all right with you, Harry, we'll start the Trooping now!' he added, in a high female voice.

Peter Cage's naval background caused him to revel in these situations and I knew he wouldn't let go until it was time to board the coach.

'Okay, lads,' he said. 'Now the old gentleman has joined us, we can go up to London to look at the Queen. On the coach, everyone!'

For the short time I had been on parade, I had stood next to my old friend Danny Cooke. He nudged me and pointed down to my shoes.

'What's the matter with your feet?'

'Eh?'

'Your feet! What's the matter with them? You've got two bloody great brass buckles on your shoes. Is something the matter with your feet?'

I looked down – Oh Christ! I saw that in my haste I had put on the wrong shoes. They were certainly clean, they were certainly black, but they each sported a large brass buckle on the outer side of the instep! The infuriating thing was, they weren't even my choice of shoes. Christine, my teenage daughter, had long been complaining about my Victorian approach to footwear and suggested that I could become a little more 'with it' in a pair of trendy shoes. Well, I was wearing my 'trendy' shoes on probably the one day in the calendar when the street coppers are thoroughly inspected!

'And where's your "M"?' piled on Danny, pointing to the district number on my shoulder.

Each policeman exhibits his or her number on the shoulder of the raincoat. Mine displayed '604' right enough, but of the letter 'M' there was no sign.

'Must have fallen off this morning,' I muttered.

'Bloody liar! It's been missing for weeks,' whispered John Charman from the row behind.

I had to admit the truth of that remark. I had placed the renewal of my letter 'M' high on my pending list of urgent tasks-to-be-completed. I had obviously not placed it high enough! My one piece of luck was that by arriving late I had missed the inspection. At least the first hurdle was cleared; one down – about a hundred to come!

I sat next to Danny on the coach, bound for an early breakfast at the police refreshment marquee in St James's Park. I was fast becoming quite concerned about my shoe buckles.

'You'll just have to lower your trousers a little,' suggested Dan.

'Oh, I'm going to look bloody marvellous, aren't I? You can imagine the Queen's conversation: "He's a smart officer, isn't he?" "Who, Your Majesty?" "Him over there. Him with no 'M' on his raincoat, brass buckles on his shoes, and his trousers at half-mast!" Oh yes, with any luck at all I'll probably make the *Royal Gazette*!'

Traffic was surprisingly heavy for a Saturday morning and our driver was compelled to make a slight detour. The journey was still, however, too short to make it worth reading, and most men whiled away the minutes by gazing out of the coach windows.

'Who was "Brussels Dawn"?' asked a young, naïve, West Country voice from the seat in front.

My knowledge of London is reasonably good, so I felt compelled to take up the query.

'Who?' I asked.

'"Brussels Dawn". She's got a statue over there,' he said.

'Sounds like a Belgium Tom who half of our regiment went through during the war,' responded Danny sleepily.

I had to confess that after a quarter of a century on the streets of London I'd never heard of Brussels Dawn. I somehow could not see a statue being erected simply because half of the rifle brigade had paid her the finest compliment they knew. I turned to follow the direction of the young recruit's pointing finger. There, on a traffic island, alongside St Martin's-in-the-Fields was a tall stone statue.

'"Brussels Dawn"!' I exploded. 'It's bloody Nurse Edith Cavell! She was a heroine from the Great War. Didn't they teach you anything at school?'

'Well, it's got "Brussels Dawn" on the base,' said the young man defensively.

'That's because she was shot at dawn in Brussels,' I explained impatiently.

'It also says "she gave herself for humanity". The same could also be said for the Rifle Brigade's Belgium Tom,' said Danny unhelpfully.

Some minutes later, our coach turned slowly into the Horse Guards Road and we all clambered out into the chill, damp, overcast morning.

Although most of my colleagues were soon pulling on their raincoats, I carried mine folded up across my arm. My cover was immediately blown by Sergeant Cage.

'If policemen were allowed to stroll around naked – you'd still manage to be improperly dressed. Get your bloody raincoat on!'

I complied.

'And where's your bloody "M"?'

'Fell off this morning, sergeant,' I lied, and, as if in proof of this story, I pulled the broken letter from my pocket.

Disbelief shone from his eyes, but then he made a clever move that showed his years of experience – he sent me to the marquee for my breakfast. In that one move he had incurred my gratitude and, temporarily at least, removed me from the scene. He, of course, would go to *his* breakfast on my return. After all, by that time the sun might be shining, then all thoughts of raincoats – and sergeants who had not inspected raincoats – could be forgotten. I walked bow-leggedly away, the bottom of my trouser legs just about covering the glint from my brass shoe-buckles.

Half an hour or so later, I emerged from the refreshment marquee. I glanced expectantly up at the sky. It had certainly stopped drizzling but the clouds were as low as ever. I groaned and slipped into my raincoat.

'It's raincoats off!' said the inspector as he advanced towards me. 'And where's your bloody "M"?'

Needless to say, the order concerning coats had been changed while I was at breakfast and now we were to remove the things.

'It fell off this morning, guv.' I again offered the offending 'M'.

'Where's your sergeant?'

'Just gone for his breakfast, guv.'

'Hmmm, well, don't forget to face the crowd when the Queen rides by!'

'Yes, guv,' I replied, and he strode quickly away.

I took up my position, appropriately in the gutter, and began to chat to some of the crowd lining the route. We were placed on the park side of Horse Guards Parade.

This meant that though we were close enough to hear the ceremony, we were not close enough actually to see it. One advantage of this position was that we could at least relax for the fifty or so minutes that the Trooping actually took.

Soon a *very* senior member of the constabulary rode precariously by on a bored-looking horse.

'Why are these men not wearing their raincoats?' he bellowed.

The inspector hurried back.

'All raincoats on!'

The *very* senior officer's eyes suddenly alighted on the vacant spot on my shoulder.

'Where's your bloody "M"?'

'Fell off this morning, guv – sir,' I answered, once more showing the blasted letter.

'Hmmm. Well, don't forget to face the crowd when the Queen rides by!'

'Sir!' I snapped dutifully.

At his third attempt, the horse moved reluctantly off.

My interest was soon taken up when the full pageantry of the Household Cavalry cantered by. I am always totally enraptured by that spectacle. I watched starry-eyed as they trotted in line abreast across the width of the road. The rattle of the harness, the steel-tipped hooves and the music of the massed bands all produce a magnificent cacophony of sound. I adore every second. They always remind me of the Errol Flynn pictures I saw when I was a boy. As the last line of troopers passed across my front, I was aware of a vigorously waving figure on the other side of the road. I removed my gaze reluctantly from the now-disappearing horses and turned instead to the dancing figure opposite. It was a superintendent and he obviously had eyes only for me. He was just waiting for a suitable gap in the procession. I somehow had the feeling he was not going to be the bearer of good news. But why? Surely not even an eagle-eyed superintendent could see my shoulder from the other side of the road? I looked bewildered up and down the road. Danny Cooke, ten yards to my right, and John Charman, an equal distance to my left, glanced sympathetically in my direction. Why were they facing in a different direction from me?

Oh no!!!

That small solitary figure that had just ridden by – was the Queen! I felt in my pocket for the 'M' and I bowed my legs till my knees hurt.

'Why didn't you face the crowd for the Queen?' he roared. 'And where's your bloody "M"!!'

'Fell off this morning, sir.' I was beginning to feel that I should have had cards printed.

He, however, made such a fuss about the missing 'M' that he seemed to forget about my royal *faux-pas*. After two full minutes of unrepeatable dialogue, he strode away scowling his very fiercest expression.

For the next fifty minutes, the sounds of the massed bands, marching and counter-marching, could be clearly heard above the hubbub of the ten-deep crowd behind me. Young children sang their own words to many of the traditional marches being played by the band. The favourite among these seemed to be the march 'The British Grenadiers'. A sweet little seven-year-old girl with a glorious Lancashire accent accompanied the musicians with the words:

There was a scotchy-lander, and he went to Waterloo.
The wind blew up his petticoat
and showed his cock-a-doodle-do,

which seemed to delight four blue-rinsed American matrons nearby.

Soon the National Anthem could be heard, and some distant commands then indicated that the ceremony was almost over. A couple more minutes and the Household Cavalry returned, this time twelve abreast. They all came to a halt just in front of me. The reason for this pause is that Princess Margaret leaves the parade ground via a different route. The cavalry then wait until she is well on her way before resuming their journey to Buckingham Palace. This 'pause' always causes a 'bottleneck' problem in Horse Guards Road. A dozen horses and riders abreast across the street tend to take up every bit of space. Policemen lining the route find there is very little room to stand – with or without their raincoats – and are therefore compelled to back firmly into the crowd until that part of the parade has passed by. A huge black gelding, some seventeen hands in height, stood twitching and tossing, barely eighteen inches in front of me.

I viewed this horse with some apprehension. I love to look at these animals but I'm not sure I like to be so close to one. I have seen elephants that have looked smaller, and those huge hooves could make an awful mess of my brass buckles. Suddenly the creature rocked forward on his front legs and splayed his rear legs out behind him. Now I may be dockland born and bred, but even I knew what that meant. The crowd behind me prevented any retreat. It did occur to me that that animal must have sunk ten barrels of real ale the night before. Another thirty seconds and I would have seriously considered requesting an ark. It absolutely flooded out. It struck the pavement with such a force that it bounced eighteen inches up again, spraying an area some four yards square.

After what seemed an eternity, the cascade finally abated. My shoes, socks, trousers and feet were saturated and I felt that my brass buckles would be lucky to escape with just a tarnish. The rider had appeared totally motionless during my drenching and remained just as immobile now it was all over. The horse itself simply turned around and stared at me. In fact he appeared to be staring straight into my eyes. He raised his great head up and down a couple of times, as if agreeing with his own good judgement. Good God, I thought, he's going to ask me where my bloody 'M' is! My hand instinctively closed over the accursed letter but a distant command caused the whole group suddenly to move off.

'I couldn't have put it better myself,' said the approaching Sergeant Cage. 'It was his opinion of your general appearance, I assume?'

I slowly looked down at my sodden feet. Then it came to me; I had just been man-managed – and by a horse! If I had deluded myself that I had won the battle of wits between myself and an assortment of senior officers, I had no doubt I had been put firmly in my place – in the gutter and pissed upon!

Usually, at the end of the Trooping ceremony the crowd slowly dissolve away. They trickle into the parks, the underground stations and the West End shops. This particular Trooping was, of course, different, being also the year of the Jubilee. As the rear of the procession finally left Horse Guards Parade to make its way along the Mall, so the crowd began involuntarily to move in behind it. The coppers lining the route swung round behind the retreating procession and formed a cushion between it and the front runners of the crowd. The advantage of this system is that the police barrier becomes larger as the numbers of the crowd increase. The disadvantage is that by the time the length of the Mall has been travelled there can be anything between one and two hundred thousand people packed in front of the Palace.

The discomfort I was experiencing from my wet feet was ceasing to be a source of humour to me. I sought out Sergeant Cage.

'Is it okay if I pop in to the refreshment tent, sarge? I must do something about my socks, they're all screwed up in my shoes.'

'They're not all that's screwed up,' he answered. 'All right, rejoin us in front of the palace.'

I began to move away.

'Oh! One other thing,' he called, 'try not to be too late, your friend the horse may want a shit!'

The crowd and the police were becoming even more tightly packed as together they shuffled their way along the Mall. I slowly edged to the side of the road and vaulted a crowd barrier that had been left in place. I then squelched my way on to the comparatively clear pavement and into St James's Park. Looking behind me, I was surprised to see I was not alone. My two colleagues, John and Danny, were just a couple of yards to my rear.

'What do you two crafty sods want?' I asked.

'We've been sent to keep an eye on you,' said John, matter-of-factly.

'I don't need "keeping an eye on", thank you. You're supposed to be looking after the Queen – not me.'

'Well,' said Dan, 'we trust the Queen; we don't bleeding trust you.'

Between the three of us, we had over eighty years' police service. There was, therefore, no way that I was going to convince these two that I wasn't just skiving off somewhere. The huge billowing tent loomed up in front of us and the first drops of rain began to fall.

We entered the marquee and at one end, stretching from one canvas wall to the other, were six empty wooden tables. This had been the food counter some two hours earlier. Other tables and benches were arranged in neat rows like pews in a church. Much more interesting was the opposite end of the tent. Here on a small table were two barrels of beer that had been supplied mainly for the assortment of voluntary helpers that such a great occasion demands.

'You lying old bugger!' said Dan.

'I didn't know, honest,' I protested.

Taking a detached view, I realized there was just no way that they were going to believe me. I knew I wouldn't have believed them if the roles had been reversed. As if to prove that sinking a pint of bitter was the last thing on my mind, I walked to the table furthest away from the two barrels and sat down. They both stood alongside me and watched in some fascination as I began to remove my shoes.

'It was your idea – so it's your round,' pronounced John, as if he was quoting from the Wisdom of Solomon.

'He's right,' weighed in Dan, putting on his impartial tone.

'Look,' I said reasonably. 'I'm not walking up to that beer counter in full uniform with no shoes and socks on! We've only got time for one pint – so let's toss for it.'

We tossed – I lost.

'Where's your shoes and socks, mate?' said the barman, making conversation while the beer trickled into our glasses.

'There was an IRA submarine in the park lake. I waded in and sunk it,' I replied casually.

'Oh,' he sniffed, and cuffed his nose with his shirt sleeve.

I turned back to our table and sat down. Both my compatriots had rolled themselves a cigarette and were as relaxed as if they had been in the lounge of some swank hotel. I slid their glasses across to them without a word. John picked up his glass and, frowning, held it up to the light.

'I think your bloody horse has been in here,' he said.

I had thought the beer was quite nice, but then I'm easily pleased.

'We'll only have time for one more, then we'll have to go,' pointed out Danny.

'Yes, I thought we might – and whose round is this one?' I asked pointedly.

‘Well, as I’m not very keen on this beer, I’ll only have half a pint. So Danny can get it,’ responded John, honestly believing he was being scrupulously fair.

I was interested to see how Danny would take this finding, and I listened to their cut and thrust on the finer points of social etiquette for some minutes. Just long enough, in fact, for the barman to have dismantled both barrels and cleared away the counter.

‘Well, come on,’ I said brusquely. ‘My feet aren’t going to become any drier, the bar’s shut and the rain’s eased off – so let’s go to the palace.’

John drained the last reluctant drop from his glass and said: ‘Pity, really, I think I could have begun to get the taste for that.’

Raising the flap of the marquee, we silently trooped across the park in search of Sergeant Cage and 200,000 people.

The Mall and the area immediately in front of the palace were unbelievable. I had never seen so many people in my life. Somehow, among that multitude, we had to find Peter Cage and twenty of our colleagues! The only clear spot within a quarter-mile in any direction from the palace was the Victoria Memorial. This memorial is a white marble structure that sits immediately in front of the palace gates. It forms the centre of a traffic roundabout and consists of fountains, steps and statues. It had been kept clear on that day, as indeed on all Royal function days, for the world’s TV cameras. We decided to make for there.

We entered the perimeter of the crowd and began to ‘excuse-me-can-I-come-by’ our way through. It took nearly twenty minutes to cover the distance but one by one we arrived at the base of the memorial steps. A brief explanation to the contingent of police guarding the place followed and we climbed the wide staircase to the top. Everywhere were duffel-coated cameramen. Their power lines were like the roots of some great forest tree that had broken the surface of the ground.

The crush in front of the palace gates was now so tight that we could only see heads. It looked a hopeless task. However, one of the camera teams, seeing our problem, lent me a pair of binoculars and I systematically scanned the crowd, section by section. Just as I had located our group – they were immediately in front of the gates – the Royal Family appeared on the balcony and a great cheer went up from the throng. It would have been physically impossible at that stage to have rejoined our beloved sergeant, so we decided to wait until the crowd thinned.

'It won't be thinning just yet,' exclaimed Dan. 'Look at that!'

I turned and looked down the Mall towards Trafalgar Square. The clouds were very low and rolling into each other like huge grey eiderdowns. Hurtling through the sky at well below cloud level was the Red Arrow Squadron. Their crimson vapour-trails streamed out behind them. They were so low and on such a straight course for the palace that we all instinctively ducked. As they rocketed off towards South Kensington, the final waves were given from the palace balcony. The drizzle became far more noticeable and the first trickles of people began to leave the crowd.

The three of us descended the memorial steps and began to filter our way through towards our colleagues. On our arrival, I realized that even they had become disorientated on the escort from Horse Guards Parade. Few of them had been able to keep together. The sheer volume of the crowd had fragmented much of the police cordon into small units. John and Danny eased their way into the group but Sergeant Cage, as usual, had eyes only for me.

He began: 'Where the hell have you been? No, don't tell

me. I suppose you didn't know the district you belonged to without the "M" on your shoulder?'

'Pressure of the crowd, sergeant. Impossible to get through.'

'Did you lose your shoes on the way, then?'

'Er, no, sergeant, why?'

'Well, the ones you're wearing look as if they came from an Oxfam shop the day after a Gay Liberation Front festival. Tell me you didn't wear those shoes this morning on parade. Tell me! Please tell me you didn't!'

'Er – I'm afraid I did, sergeant.'

He closed his eyes, lifted up his head and whimpered, apparently to the sky, 'He did.' Opening his eyes, he turned to me once again. 'All that fuss about your bloody "M" by all those senior officers and you're telling me that the whole time you were wearing two bloody great buckles on your shoes?'

'Yes, sergeant.'

'The inspector! The superintendent! The deputy assistant commissioner! The Queen!' he moaned.

'I don't think the Queen minded, sergeant,' I said, trying to calm the troubled waters.

'No! She probably thought you were the new bloody court jester. What'll you wear next year? A cap and bells? Perhaps a pig's bladder on a stick?'

We strode down the Mall to pick up our coach from Horse Guards Road. There were still numerous senior police officers about. Each time we passed one, I had to bow my legs in order to cover the buckles, much to the obvious delight of my colleagues. 'This town's not big enough for both of us, marshal' or 'You've got till sundown to get outa town, sheriff' were just two of the many remarks I bore with fortitude.

Forty-five minutes later, we were standing at the saloon bar in the Duke of Sutherland. I watched in eager anticipation as big Jean drew up a foaming pint.

'Well, d'you boys have a nice time seeing the Queen?' she asked.

'Yes,' answered Dan, 'very good indeed. We saw the parade. We almost took the salute on the fly-past. John and I had a free pint – and a horse pissed on Harry. All in all I think it was a very good Trooping indeed.'

The Market

Elsewhere in this book, I wrote that with the exception of the Labour Party Headquarters, Wharf Road is somewhat short of famous buildings or locations. On reflection that is an injustice. In reality, hardly anyone visits the Labour Party Headquarters, other than for a specific purpose. We do, on the other hand, have another location where thousands attend every week, for no reason other than it is there. This place is East Street market, or 'the Lane' as it is more commonly known. Parts of the Lane are open most of the week, the climax of business building up to a Sunday morning peak. Many traders do not in fact attend at all between Monday to Friday, concentrating all their efforts on the whole of Saturday and Sunday.

Almost anything can be purchased in East Street and it usually is. If one takes into account the various sidestreets, where unofficial little markets sprout up from time to time, then its overall length is well over half a mile. Easily ten thousand people will be in attendance at any one time on a Sunday morning, with that figure soaring to nearer 30,000 in the weekends before Christmas. At that time of the year, the throng is so huge that stalls have been turned over by the sheer volume of people. In the main street, most of the traders are licensed by the council; in the sidestreets, in doorways and vacant lots, this law does not apply. Strictly speaking, anyone who trades in the streets of Southwark without a licence from the council is breaking the law. Those who break it with the greatest regularity are the 'fly-pitchers'. These gentlemen usually operate from suitcases on the junction corners and street doorways. They sometimes employ a look-out, rather in the manner of the old-fashioned street bookmaker. Like their bookmaking predecessors, they are arrested with some regularity. Not regular enough, though, according to the legitimate traders who have to pay their rates and licence fees. In addition there are kids who get the barrows and handcarts out for the stallholders, before the market opens; also the dustmen who clear up once it has closed. Floating around with some irregularity are the 'dips' (pickpockets); lost children; political hooligans; Crown and Anchor and Find the Lady teams.

Long before I had ever thought of joining the Metropolitan Police, I had an affinity with the market. My father, for example, was one of a typical Victorian family of a dozen kids. He lived close by the Lane and the family was so large that they were compelled to rent two small adjoining houses. The main advantage of renting two houses was that one also acquired two backyards. All sorts of things could be kept in backyards. In my father's case it was a goat! Where better to sell a Walworth-born goat than in East Street market? In recounting this story to me, my father carefully omitted any mention of smell. Nor even the reaction of neighbours – truly the great unwashed!

Even from my own childhood, I have fond memories of the Lane. In those days, before the last war, the market would be open until late on a Saturday night. The traders would work by gas-flares. As a child, walking down the market with my parents, I would be given a special Saturday night treat. This usually took the form of a jelly. Not a jelly that had been diluted into some cissy-shaped mould, but a real, raw jelly straight from the packet. This raspberry-flavoured rubber could be chewed for hours.

Once I had left school and begun to earn money of my own, my pal Bill and I would promenade down East Street market every Sunday morning. All we ever bought was a choc-ice! We bought them winter and summer, come rain or snow, sunshine or fog. We would thread our way through the milling thousands simply to buy an ice that we could have purchased at the local shop barely two minutes' walk from home. Without even realizing it, we had become part of the South London Sunday morning ritual of 'going dahn the Lane'. It was with this market background that I first came to Wharf Road as a recruit nearly thirty years ago.

Although police stations all look very much alike, they differ in both character and atmosphere. One station will almost specialize in one sort of offence, while another, with a very similar geography, will barely scratch the surface of it. Tradition plays a great part in this. In theory we all dress the same, look the same and carry out the same laws. Therefore the end result should be more or less identical. In practice, it is anything but. If stations are so different, then it would be true to say that people in charge of them, be they chief inspectors, superintendents or chief superintendents, have an even greater variety of approach. In the main, East Street market has been treated by successive Wharf Road guv'nors with a policy of laissez-faire. Every decade or so, however, one will arrive and decide that the market is an unlawful shambles – which it sometimes can be – and it was about time it was cleaned up.

The biggest law-enforcing problem with the market is its very size. Take the question of obstruction. Any location with between ten and thirty thousand people milling around in the street is an obstruction in itself. The entire bloody market constitutes an obstruction. There are certain bye-laws that can cover parts of this difficulty but they make no allowances for even the simplest everyday problems. For example: stallholders' boxes should not be on the pavement – but they need to sit occasionally. Spaces between the stalls are clearly defined by law – but many goods that are offered for sale simply overlap the barrow. Trading must cease at 1 p.m. on Sundays – but what can you do when twenty or thirty people are gathered around a stall and wishing to buy? The street itself is one-way – how can you get your goods delivered if the van arrives at the wrong end? Junctions should be kept clear – but stallholders constantly need to replenish their stock, therefore their vehicle needs always to be accessible. Every transaction made in the streets of Southwark, except from a licensed stall, is almost certainly unlawful – yet is a traditional London market, a century old. Those are just a few of the problems for police to interpret. The laws are framed for the public at large. It is this very public who requires these markets. It is a very fine balance indeed.

My own arrival at Wharf Road was preceded by a few months by Superintendent Hall. As far as many old traders were concerned, Hall was a greater disaster for the market than Adolf Hitler. He was in reality an extremely fair-minded man, he just did not understand the problems of the traders or their ways. Each Sunday morning at 7 a.m., two hours before the market could expect to begin any business, each junction would be patrolled by one, sometimes two, uniformed policemen. Junctions would be kept clear for seventy-five yards back from East Street. Unlicensed trading was never allowed even to begin. Barrow spaces were checked, stalls would be lined up, selling would cease promptly at 1 p.m. – and the complaints flooded in.

Jim Hall was a striking figure in every way. He stood six feet two inches high, he sported an enormous, thick moustache, and when out of uniform he wore a large, fawn-coloured, camel-hair overcoat. He never yelled or threw a tantrum, but he had a cold, clinical way of dealing with subordinates that left them in no doubt as to who was in charge. If ever he had cause to admonish a man, he would do so in a tone that surgeons reserve for telling you they are about to take your leg off – and, he was about as much fun. Even his nickname was respectful, 'Jimmy-the-One'. There was only one Jimmy – and we had him! He knew, everyone knew, that he was destined for very high things and that Wharf Road was just a temporary halt in this progress. If Jim Hall said the market was a mess – then the market was a mess. All a recruit could do was to grit his teeth and hope that promotion soon caused a change of regime.

On my first Sunday morning on duty down the Lane, I was posted to the junction of East Street and Brandon Street. Fifteen yards away on the opposite side of the road was another constable, Taff Stone, a red-faced Welshman with over twenty years' service. By 11 a.m. we had already received two visits from Jimmy-the-One. Each time, I had failed to see him approach. The first I was aware of his presence was when I heard a cold cultured voice ask: 'Everything all right, Cole?'

'Er-yes, yes, sir!'.

'Then why is this linoleum all over the road?' he almost whispered.

At that particular junction stood the lino stall. The trader, in an effort to display his wares, would, from time to time, unroll a spool of lino up the middle of the road. This caused an even greater crush on the pavement.

'Oh! Is it, sir? Er – sorry about that. I never saw it.' (I couldn't very well admit that I had spent so much time looking for Jimmy himself that I was never in with a chance of seeing the lino.)

'You did not see it, Cole?'

'No, sir.'

'But it is totally blocking the road.'

'Er- yes, sir, so it is, sir.'

'And it is ten yards long and only six feet in front of you.'

'So it is, sir.'

'Are your eyes all right, Cole?'

'Fine, sir.'

'Well, if you open them a bit wider, you may see the stallholder. Keep them open long enough and you may be able to summons him before they close again.'

With that, both Jimmy and his camel-hair coat were gone. It was always a constant source of wonder to me, how he could appear and disappear as if by magic.

I may not have seen Jimmy appear, but I was aware of each of Taff Stone's movements, as he threaded his way through the crowd, from across the street.

'What'd he want, boyo?'

'He just gave me a bollicking about the lino in the road. Said I've got to summons the bloke,' I replied, in the matter-of-fact-manner that I thought an experienced copper might adopt.

'Where'd he go?' persisted Taff.

'Dunno, down towards the bottom end of the market, I think.'

'Hmmmmmm,' murmured Taff to no one in particular. 'Come with me, boyo.'

Taff walked me to a large covered van that was parked about thirty yards from the junction.

'In you go,' he said.

I looked at him questioningly for a moment, but when you are a brand-new recruit and an old copper says 'In you go', well, in you go.

'Right, sit there.' He pointed to an old wooden box. 'And keep your eyes open!'

Ah, action at last! I thought. I suppose we're watching out for pickpockets or suchlike. I studied intently the junction I had just left. Not that I could see much of it, the lino man had just laid another spool!

'Here y'are, boyo,' said Taff heartily, thrusting a quart of brown ale and a basin of jellied eels in my hands!

'Yuk! What's that?'

'Jellied eels! You're a local boy and you don't know jellied eels when you see them?'

'I know jellied eels right enough. I just don't like 'em. Just the sight of 'em makes me feel sick.'

'Give them to me then, boyo. I'll show you how to eat them. You just get on and drink your beer.'

'But I don't drink brown ale.'

Taff looked at me incredulously.

'You, a Londoner born and bred and don't drink brown ale *and* you don't eat jellied eels?' His eyes narrowed and, moving closer to me, he studied me intently. 'You're not one of them homosexuals, are you?' he added suspiciously.

''Course I'm not,' I protested. 'I'm quite sure that somewhere in London are many queers that could live contentedly for the rest of their lives on nothing else but eels and brown ale. I happen not to like them, neither am I homosexual.'

'Well, get out of the van then and keep a watch out for Jimmy,' he snapped.

I almost fell out of the van in my haste to escape from the eels, and within seconds I had resumed my place on the street corner.

'Where is PC Stone, Cole?' murmured Jimmy-the-One, as he emerged seemingly from a crack in the pavement.

'He's – er, he's checking on that lorry, sir. He said I hadn't been here long enough to know the traders so he has gone to find out who it belongs to.'

'Has he now? Well, there is an unfortunate fellow just around the corner, who has just had a fit. He also appears to be somewhat infested with vermin. I think PC Stone could deal with that situation quite satisfactorily. Do you not agree?'

Only too eager to share an opinion with a superintendent, I readily agreed that Police Constable Stone would indeed be absolutely perfect for such an incident. Just at that moment Taff emerged from the rear of the van. Jimmy glided smoothly over to him. Taff's usual red face changed to a flushed purple but I could not make out any details of the conversation. They both made their way into the mainstream of the crowd and were soon lost to sight.

I remained practically motionless on that corner until the crowd faded and the traders began to clear away. The lino man began to carry his unsold rolls of linoleum towards the same lorry in which I had offended Taff. He slid in the first two rolls then, reaching inside, he removed two paper cartons and a couple of empty beer bottles.

''Ere, look at this, guv'nor,' he called to me. 'These bleedin' vagrants get everywhere.'

No wonder Taff was purple! He had obviously been faced with the choice of leaving his 'elevenses' in the van, probably indefinitely, or swallowing the lot before Jimmy arrived at the rear of the lorry. In the six minutes that it took me to leave the van and meet the superintendent on the corner of the market, he had demolished two cartons of jellied eels and sunk four pints of brown ale! There was no doubt about it, those old pre-war coppers were a race apart.

Some six months later, I strolled down the Lane on a beautiful autumn Sunday morning. The warm September sunshine had placed me in a relaxed mood. A short dapper man was standing on a barrow auctioning off bunches of fruit. He fired out the words of his sales spiel with the velocity of a machine-gun.

'I'm-not-asking-five-pounds, not-four-not-three-not-two-pounds, not-even-one-pound. 'Ere, I'm in a generous mood – fifteen shillings! No, wait a minute! It is my mother's birthday today – 'ere, half-a-quid! Lady over there!'

He pointed twice vaguely towards the rear of the crowd. This was the signal for the more impulsive buyers at the front to panic. Up went their arms. Finally twenty or more people were standing on tip-toe with an arm upstretched like primary school children trying to catch the teacher's eye. Seeing me passing by, he broke from his usual sales banter.

'No wonder you're looking so pleased,' he called out. 'He's going, ain't he?'

'Who's going?' I asked in genuine puzzlement.

'Jimmy-the-One, a'course. Nah then, who'd like this bloody great bunch for only a quid?'

That was my first introduction to the East Street grapevine. Every trader in the market knew about the superintendent's impending departure, long before the police personnel at the station ever did. So Jimmy was going at last? Well, Sundays should now be happier for everyone, at least for a while.

That Sunday, I was making my way to the bottom end of the market where the public meetings were held. Usually there were about four of these meetings. They were held at the junction of East Street and Dawes Street. Two meetings would be held simultaneously, out of sight of each other and just around the corner. One advantage of this system was that both meetings could be supervised by a solitary PC standing on the corner. Each of the four organizations holding the meetings would decide among themselves exactly in what order they would speak. This was accomplished in a very civilized manner and police would only be concerned in a conciliatory capacity, should any of the parties disagree. These parties consisted usually of the Communist Party, the Socialist Party of Great Britain (no connection at all with the Labour Party), the Ex-Servicemen's Movement for Peace (now, I believe, extinct) and usually a religious organization, the denomination of which would vary, but would often be Methodist.

The task of supervising the meetings was not everyone's cup of tea, but on a pleasant day I would quite enjoy it. By far and away my favourite would be the Communist Party. This preference was due exclusively to the charisma of its regular Sunday speaker, one Joe Bent. Joe was a marvellous street orator. I never saw him use a microphone yet his voice would be heard clearly above the general hubbub of the rest of the market. Whereas the other meetings tended to be repetitive, the same subjects endlessly discussed, Joe would use a current news topic and milk it potentially for all its worth. One fist would punctuate every fighting syllable, while the other thumped his platform of steps in an alternate counterpoint. Joe was a splendid sight indeed, with a thick mane of grey hair. The others suffered sadly in comparison. He would make the most scathing attacks on the police force, yet would treat the PC on duty at the meetings with the utmost courtesy. Again, the same could not always be said for his rivals.

There was one very strict discipline rule concerning the policing of those meetings. On no account were they to be left unpoliced. Even an urgent visit to the toilet was not considered a suitable excuse. It was claimed that the constable should remain in position until a colleague wandered by. The newcomer could then take over at the meeting until the appointed officer returned. This was not without its difficulties. Supposing nature's call was urgent and did not manifest itself until thirty seconds after a colleague had actually passed by? Jimmy-the-One's rules made no allowance for the previous evening's social life. Four pints of bitter and a plate of whelks were never in Jim Hall's Saturday programme; therefore, he could not understand why it should be on anyone else's.

Perhaps because I spent more time than most on speakers' corner, I developed my own system for leaving the place. It was almost infallible; it was called 'Lost Children'. The Lane absolutely abounds with lost children. I often feel that forty per cent of all parents visiting the market do so with the deliberate intention of losing their kids. On the other hand, some of the kids I have found have made it very obvious why their parents should wish to lose them in the first place. How else can one explain two- and three-year-olds being allowed to wander freely around and trampled underfoot?

'I've lost my little girl, officer.'

'When did you last see the child, sir?'

'About a couple of hours ago at the top end of the lane.'

'How old is she, sir?'

'She'll be three next week.'

A cryptic 'You don't think she's taken the car and driven straight home, do you, sir?' will invariably pass straight over his head.

In spite of all the tribulations that a lost child can bring, they were always handy for a good twenty minutes away from the meetings. Sometimes they would be upset, sometimes they would be overweight. If they were upset and overweight, then there was indeed a problem. I once carried a distressed five-year-old hippo half a mile back to the station one Sunday morning. I did not fully recover until the Wednesday afternoon.

Gradually, some time during the mid-sixties, speakers' corner just faded quietly away. Joe Bent moved from the district, and without its star turn the old corner had no character any more. In the last two years, though, politics have moved back into our street market. They are not the politics of the street, however, as much as of the gutter. This time it is a whole different set-up. There is no pre-match discussion by all the parties concerned. There is none of the respect for each other's views, as there was in previous years. In fact there is nothing at all, really, just a boring mutual hatred by the Socialist Workers' Party and the National Front. They hurl their idealistic rhetoric to the complete indifference of passers-by. They hold no meetings; they have no question-time. Few of them are capable of any intelligent verbal communication anyway. Joe Bent could draw a crowd, sometimes of more than a hundred people. All that his successors can manage is a handful of skinheads and a few thirty-year-old sociology students. Intellectually, they all have difficulty understanding the push-button pedestrian crossing.

The location of these political parties has also changed. Originally it was situated at the bottom end of the market outside the Family Planning Clinic, with just one copper in attendance. Most visitors would have to battle through half a mile of crowded market even to reach the place. With today's demand for publicity, they have moved to the top end of the Lane. Here, at the junction with Walworth Road, they stand zombie-like, offering for sale their poisonous news sheets with half a dozen coppers in attendance. A sad aspect of this change is that it is now the casual visitor's first glimpse of the market itself.

Other than these early eyesores, the market is well worth a trip. In the main, the goods offered for sale are excellent value. After all, they are there openly displayed for all to see and usually the trader has been established in the market for several years. There are of course exceptions. The 'fly-pitchers', for example; here today and gone tomorrow. These fellows will work almost every market in London and the surrounding counties. They frequently intimate that their goods are stolen property, hence their low price. This draws the unwary even more; there is nothing like getting someone else's property cheaply.

Although many of these fly-pitchers are arrested with some regularity, on the whole I found them to be an amusing and colourful bunch. One rather large Wharf Road constable who had, at least in their eyes, been very overbearing, was christened Yogi Bear. Two days before Christmas, an enormous box of sugar puffs was delivered anonymously at the station counter. It bore the simple inscription: 'To Yogi'.

These boys are really at their best with some of their own names: 'Dennis the Brain'; 'Tony Doughnuts'; 'Suss-ie Sid'; 'Pump-iron Bryan'; and my two favourites, 'Monkey' and 'Grand'. The latter two were so-called because they always talked of money in high-finance terms. Every transaction they ever made always seemed to cost a 'Monkey' (£500) or a 'Grand' (£1000). Unfortunately, they have recently gone bust. Now, I hear, they are referred to as 'Pony' (£25) and 'Pennies'!

One of the many recurring complaints the police received about the fly-pitchers was their extraordinary inability to label their articles clearly. Every Christmas a procession of people would call at the Wharf Road counter to complain that they had been fleeced.

'I bought this bottle of rum down the Lane; it's nuffink like bloody rum – it's awful!'

'How much did you pay for it?'

'Er-well, 'arf a quid.'

'You expect good rum for half a quid? Look at the print at the bottom of the label.'

There was the large word 'RUM' followed by the small words – 'flavoured cordial'.

Our other regular yule-tide visitor, in addition to Santa Claus, was the 'Christmas tree man'. For the three weeks prior to the great day, he would sell his trees in the market. He would, of course, need to plan his purchases and hire a large lorry, but come 25 December, any trees remaining unsold were just left in the street. He would then disappear for another eleven and a half months.

Half-way down the Lane stood a sad little stall. It

contained a dozen or so assorted bottles of liniment and a scattering of yellow photographs. The photographs were of its owner, one Tommy Noble, a former bantam-weight champion of Great Britain. Tommy now stood in the gutter each weekend, supplementing his income by selling rubbing oils. Almost incoherently punch drunk, he would willingly relive old fights for anyone wishing to purchase a bottle of liniment. Tommy was a sad little monument to the cruelties of the fight game.

Before a copper has performed many Sunday duties down the Lane, he is almost certain to run across some poor soul who requires an ambulance. It could be as the result of an accident, or an assault, although it is more likely to be caused by a physical condition, aggravated by the massed crowd. Experience will soon teach that officer of the need to give explicit instructions when he telephones ambulance control. Exact directions for approaching via sidestreets are vital. On my first call to the ambulance service, I simply gave the location as East Street, followed by the nearest shop number. All local ambulances were unfortunately engaged. The patient and I had to wait while an ambulance was summoned from Victoria, a few miles away. The only location the crew had to refer to was 'outside number 201 East Street, SE17'. They studied the map and understandably decided to travel via the main roads, to avoid becoming lost. As a result, we waited an hour and ten minutes for the ambulance to travel three miles. It had arrived at the top end of the Lane within six minutes. It spent the next hour negotiating the last half-mile through 10,000 shoppers. The ambulance inflicted as many casualties on that trip as it conveyed to hospital in the remainder of its working life.

I suppose a casual visitor may have wondered why there was a need to call an ambulance in the first place. The market had two 'doctors' in regular attendance each Sunday. These marvellous gentlemen were a couple of first-class quacks. Their sales-talk fascinated me for many hours. The entire stock of medicine of one of them consisted of hundreds of little green vitamin pills and a few dozen bars of plain white washing soap. Wearing a white coat and carrying a stethoscope, his line was roughly as follows: if it was an inside job, i.e., appendicitis, gall-stones or cancer, then the pills would do the trick. If it was an outside job, i.e., dermatitis, chilblains or first-degree burns, then apply the soap. He would claim that he sold his wares for a pittance in the market place, purely as an act of charity.

'However,' he would state severely, 'if you wish to avail of my services in my Harley Street consulting rooms, then you must be prepared to pay my Harley Street fees. If, on the other hand, you have a personal medical problem which you do not wish to express here in public, then I will be in the saloon bar of the Masons Arms from 1.15 p.m. onwards.'

Always an excellent place for medical research was the saloon bar of the 'Masons', especially around closing time.

The incredible thing was, people would positively swear by his pills and soaps. They would purchase them year after year. There was never a shortage of clients to give personal testimonials; he always had dozens of letters piled high on his stall. The fact that each one of them would have recovered as quickly if they'd applied chicken shit and borax was never considered. His failures, of course – those who took vitamin pills for terminal illnesses – were never around long enough to complain. He was on a winner all the way. Even during the weekdays when he resumed his job as a second-hand-car salesman.

For those who do not feel in need of urgent surgery, but nevertheless are suffering from a jaded stagnation, there is of course the 'tonic stall'. This stall, in various guises, has been established in the market for generations. The stall owner will pour, from a large bottle, an interesting yellowy liquid, usually into small, sherry-like glasses. Customers then boldly approach the stall and, picking up the glass in one sweeping fluid movement, they down the contents in a swift gulp (sure indication to me that it probably tastes foul). While never having the courage to try the contents for myself, I once asked a friend about its taste and why he drank it.

'It tastes like quinine to me, and I drink it 'cos it's good fer yer,' he answered blandly.

'But why is it good for yer?' I persisted.

He thought deeply for a moment, then said: 'Well it just is, that's all.'

Which, as far as the customer is concerned, is all that really matters.

The quack doctors and the tonic stalls were places for many young police recruits, fresh from their remote villages, to learn of the curious ways of the big city. They were not, however, locations that would present them with many problems in the course of their actual duty. Not like the second-hand-cycle dealers, for example. At the bottom end of the market, where the lines of stalls finish and the crowd thins out, small groups of men gather. Propped against the kerb just in front of them are usually a line of assorted cycles. The prospective vendors of these machines are a mixed bunch. Most are the owners of a bike which they simply wish to sell. Some are part-time dealers. These men carry out a job of work during the week and refurbish old cycles as a hobby. Some are simply thieves. Occasionally the police will mount a cycle swoop. This takes the form of a few policemen rounding up all the machines and checking the manufacturers' number against the record of cycles stolen. This can prove interesting. While checking the number of a blue Raleigh cycle one Sunday, I noticed that the paint underneath the saddle was in fact red. The number was also on our stolen list. I invited the eighteen-year-old 'owner' to accompany me to the station to assist with my enquiries. Half an hour or so later I called upon his mother to tell her that her son would be engaged for a while.

'I'm sure it's a mistake,' she said. ''E's a good boy really. 'E'd never take anyfing that didn't belong to 'im, honest 'e wouldn't.'

In his bedroom that measured little more than eleven foot square was a single bed, two lockers, one wardrobe, one dressing-table and the major parts of fourteen stolen cycles!

'How about these bloody bikes, then?' I asked.

'Oh, yer. I've seen 'em, I just fort he was interested in bikes,' she said disarmingly.

'He is, other people's bikes.'

Stolen cycles are not, of course, the only crime problems in the market. Two of the most distressing are 'dipping' and 'snatching'. In the former, a crook literally dips into anything that may be of value. The term originally applied to pickpockets, who are often quite highly skilled. It has taken on a new meaning and now applies as much to groups of scavenging kids as to any criminal artistes. In spite of numerous publicity campaigns, vast numbers of women still carry their purses in their shopping bags providing food and drink to the dips.

Even more distressing than the 'dip' victims, are the victims of the 'snatchers'. The more elderly and infirm the victim is, the more they are usually taken for. Very many working-class folk of the older generation do not use banks. They either mistrust them, or feel that their savings are too small to be of interest to any big bank or building society. One of the saddest tasks I ever undertook was to commiserate with an eighty-year-old widow who had just lost her entire life-savings of £400. The money had been in a purse that had just been ripped from her arthritic fingers, by a couple of laughing teenage boys. The lady was in the process of being rehoused from an old Walworth slum into a brand-new flat. She had taken her money from the top of her wardrobe to buy some new furniture. How does one even begin to console a person in these circumstances? It is no use saying: 'You should have put it in a bank.' That doesn't recover a single penny. The victim's reaction is often one of total numbness. After that they want to die. Many in fact do. It would be of interest to research just how many elderly victims of crime die of 'natural causes' within a few months of their attack.

Dipping and snatching tend to appear in bursts. For months the market will be relatively free of street crime, then a small team will move into the area and the crime figures begin to escalate. I will long remember one tired detective, at the time of the 1980 Olympics.

'They ought'a have a new event,' he said. 'We could enter a team just from the market.'

'What'll it be called?' I asked.

'How about "The snatch and flee"?' he suggested wearily.

Crime in fact tends to play little part in the day-to-day running of the market. On the other hand, verbal complaints to policemen can run quite high. Licensed traders complain about fly-pitchers, local residents complain about the general nuisance, disgruntled shoppers complain about faulty merchandise, ladies complain that they cannot use the public toilet – because other ladies are trying on dresses! All of these, plus the ever-recurring problem of street parking. To visit East Street market is to see the average motorist at the very peak of his stupidity. The area is an absolute maze of sidestreets. Anyone prepared to walk for five or six minutes can park comfortably. If they were prepared to walk for ten minutes they could have a street to themselves! Unfortunately, the usual thinking is to drive right up to the market, then begin to look for that elusive six yards of kerb-space. The result is chaos. I have often felt that good money could be made out of hiring sloping frames. In this way, some car drivers could actually park on the roof of other cars. After all, they park everywhere else. They park on pavements, driveways, fire exits, factory gates, junctions, pedestrian crossings, middle of the road and even, on one occasion, in the black Maria bay in the police station yard! To summons such a motorist is to guarantee one of the two following replies:

1. 'But I was only here for a minute.'

A recruit will soon realize that no motorist in the history of the internal combustion engine has ever admitted parking anywhere for more than one minute.

The second reply is possibly the most illogical response that any police officer will ever have to cope with.

2. 'Why aren't you out catching the murderers/rapists? I had an aunt/uncle/sister/brother/cocker spaniel/god-mother, who was raped/murdered. Why aren't you catching them, eh? Tell me that.'

During the second reply, the recruit will learn that every motorist who parks for only sixty seconds in a prohibited area will have at least one relative who has been either raped or murdered.

The market, then, is a complete hotch-potch. Every aspect of London can be found within it. It is said that if you stroll down East Street when the market is open, you will always see someone you know. This is no myth. A young West Country recruit, on his first day in the market, self-consciously made his way through a crowd of people in a shop doorway. Sitting on a chair in a rather distressed condition was an old white-haired man.

'He just came over bad and we sat him down,' said the shopkeeper anxiously.

'I'm all right,' whispered the old chap. 'Just get me a taxi.'

Now distressed old gentlemen in East Street market do

not usually travel by cab. There was also something very familiar about the old chap's face. Well, it wasn't every day that a policeman could assist Charlie Chaplin, as the old star searched for his childhood haunts.

A hundred years ago, the local coppers from Wharf Road would patrol the market in exactly the same way that they do today. The market doesn't change. It ignores cissy arcades, plastic supermarkets and confusing hypermarkets. Chaplin may have gone, together with the quacks, Dad's goat and the lino-man, but little else has altered. It survived the blitz and Jimmy-the-One; it will doubtless survive my retirement!

Harry Cole

POLICEMAN'S PROGRESS

Being one of four policemen coping with the drunken, sex-mad, middle-aged, pear-shaped Clara, or sitting out a night with the neighbourhood ghost, or calming wayward Rosie, the local prostitute, who'd had her 'Bristols' bitten, must have been a lot more fun than digging out the late and seventy-year-old Elsie Morton, rotting in bed after not being seen for some weeks, dealing with violence, or bearing the news of fatal accidents to bereaved families.

PC Harry Cole, now nearly thirty years on the Southwark force, has done it all and there's consequently many a tale to tell. He produces his account of life on the beat with a combination of good humour and honesty that makes *Policeman's Progress* a rich mixture of riotous and serious reading. Harry Cole's loyalty to the force, but also his obvious sympathy for all reasonable human eccentricities, make one feel that he would be a good man to have around when there's trouble.

A Grain of Truth

Jack Webster

In this autobiography by one of Scotland's best known journalists Jack Webster writes vividly of his childhood in Aberdeenshire, of golden hairsts and feein' markets, of honest toil and twinkling humour – the beginning of a route which took him from the *Turriff Advertiser* to the *Scottish Daily Express*.

He writes of his meetings with the rich and famous, from Charlie Chaplin to Mohammed Ali, and of his coverage of great events. But through it all Jack Webster remains a man of the North East, firmly rooted in his origins and their very real values.

FONTANA PAPERBACKS

Helen Forrester

TWOPENCE TO CROSS THE MERSEY

Helen Forrester tells the sad but never sentimental story of her childhood years, during which her family fell from genteel poverty to total destitution. In the depth of the Depression, mistakenly believing that work would be easier to find, they moved from the South of England to the slums of Liverpool. Here Helen Forrester, the eldest of seven children, experienced the worst degradations that being poor can bring. She writes about them without self-pity but rather with a rich sense of humour which makes her account of these grim days before the Welfare State funny as well as painful.

'The clarity with which utter privation is here recorded is of a rare kind' – Gillian Reynolds, *Guardian*

'. . . records, with remarkable steadiness and freedom from self-pity, the story of a childhood that – even if it was all forty years ago – most people would have set down in rage and despair' – Edward Blishen, *Books and Bookmen*

'. . . her restraint and humour in describing this stark history make it all the more moving' – *Daily Telegraph*